EVERYDAY INITIATIONS

EVERYDAY
INITIATIONS

HOW EVERY MOMENT IS INITIATING YOU TO
BE YOUR BEST SELF

ANNE VAN DE WATER

Waterside Press

Printed in the United States of America
First Printing, 2019
ISBN-13: 978-1-941768-69-3 print edition
ISBN-13: 978-1-939116-26-0 e-book edition

Waterside Press
2055 Oxford Ave
Cardiff, CA 92007
www.waterside.com

WELCOME

This is an Initiation.

An Initiation is a Rite of Passage.

It is a journey of crossing the threshold from an old way of being into a new way of being.

Initiations, like Rites of Passage, mark a major shift from one age or stage of life to the next.

Initiations happen for many reasons.

Joyous Initiations include birth, birthdays, coming of age, graduation, marriage, anniversaries, moving into or buying a new home, starting a new business or going on a Vision Quest.

Challenging Initiations include the death of a loved one or your own death process, illness, accidents, natural disasters, the ending of a friendship, relationship or marriage, divorce, your children leave the nest, or a business or financial investment that didn't turn out how you planned.

Oftentimes Initiations are prompted because you just feel like something is off in your life and you know you have to make some big changes if you are going to feel aligned, congruent and on the right path for your Soul.

During life's many Initiations you are invited to let go of what you know and what may have up until this moment felt safe and comfortable.

To release your attachment to the familiar can bring up feelings of fear and insecurity.

Oftentimes in these moments, even though it can feel scary, it is worth facing the fear because you have received a deep call from your Soul.

Your Soul is asking you to let go of who you no longer are and what no longer serves you so that you can step fully into the light of your truest, deepest and highest Self.

You have to be willing to lose who you thought you were in order to birth a new way of being where you feel a new sense of belonging, home, safety and deep connection to your Soul's deepest essence.

Initiations require you to come face to face with the unknown and The Great Mystery.

If you are paying attention and are devoted to your Soul's path, you will notice that in between life's big Initiations, there are lots of EVERYDAY INITIATIONS with every person, place and thing in your presence. In fact, every moment is initiating you to be your best self.

No matter what Initiation you are going through right now, be it joyful or challenging, internally or externally activated, know that it is helping you to grow.

And it is oftentimes the most challenging and harrowing Initiations, that when embraced, help you evolve the most as a human being and as a Soul.

The truth is, if you are on a devoted spiritual path, you are always transforming.

You are always releasing what no longer serves you and embracing who you are now.

You are always moving out of the darkness and into the light.

And life is constantly initiating you to be who you truly are.

Whatever Initiations you are currently going through big or small, know that you are not alone.

The Great Mystery, Great Spirit and the Light of your Soul are leading, guiding, directing and protecting you every step of the way.

And as Winston Churchill said:

If you are going through Hell, keep going.

And I would like to add:

If you are flowing through Heaven, keep flowing.

There is great freedom and fulfillment awaiting you on the other side.

I love you and I support you.

DEDICATION

For Gay Hendricks for believing in me and being my Earth Angel.

For Eric Van de Water for loving and supporting me from the Spirit World and being my Guardian Angel.

I love you.

I support you.

I am grateful for you.

CONTENTS

FOREWORD

Gay Hendricks, Ph.D.

A while back an e-newsletter caught my attention, written by a woman named Anne Van de Water. Many such newsletters come into my in-box every month, but this one was something special. It addressed a subject of eternal interest to any seeker—initiation—but it was the style of her writing that most enchanted me. The essay was a deeply personal story about an epic journey of suffering and liberation, and along the way the power of her words showed me something about initiation I hadn't seen before.

After reading her first newsletter, I began to look forward to them, even growing impatient when she hadn't sent out one in a while. Each piece I read was a carefully-crafted jewel. Here was a person who was using her words as an art form, almost as if she was creating paintings in space. To encounter this quality of writing is sufficiently rare that it inspired me to send Anne a note of appreciation. We struck up a correspondence, which led to my suggestion that she write a book. I am happy that she followed through with such a beautiful one.

Although I've only met Anne in person on a couple of occasions, I feel like I know her, through the heart-full clarity of her writing, as well as I know many friends of long-standing. As you appreciate this book, I suggest you make the journey a leisurely one, just as you might take a walk with a good friend. Take time to savor Anne's language and the way she weaves insights into her stories. I predict you will find your relationship with Anne to be entertaining, mindful and heart-expanding.

"Hide God in the humans.
They will never think to look there."

—*Greek Mythology*

"It is probable that the next Buddha will not take
the form of an individual. The next Buddha may
take the form of a community, a community
practicing understanding and loving kindness,
a community practicing mindful living. This may be
the most important thing we can do for the survival
of the earth."

—*Thich Nhat Hanh*

"To feel the intimacy of brothers (and sisters) is
a marvelous thing in life. To feel the love of people
whom we love is a fire that feeds our life. But to feel
the affection that comes from those whom we do
not know, that is something still greater and more
beautiful because it widens out the boundaries of
our being, and unites all living things."

—*Pablo Neruda*

EVERYDAY INITIATIONS

I know what you want.

It's what we all want deep down inside.

You want to feel like you are fully alive, present and connected.

You want to feel like your life is infused with Soul, Spirit and magic.

You want to feel like you are living from your Heart and that you are giving and receiving Love every day.

You want to feel like every day is amazing, that your life truly matters and that you are truly making a difference.

You want to feel like you are a good person and that you are creating good vibes in the world.

You want to feel like you are the best you that you can possibly be every day.

You want to feel like you are constantly growing and evolving as a human being and as spiritual being.

You want connection. True connection.

Connection with who you truly are.

Connection with your loved ones.

Connection with everyone and everything in your presence.

Because when you don't feel connected internally and externally, then life can feel very lonely and meaningless.

The Truth is, every moment is a moment when true connection is possible.

But something doesn't feel right.

And you can feel it.

You and everyone else in the world has been taught that things have to be a special way on some special day in some special place for whatever you are doing and being to be truly special.

The basic false belief that is operating in most of the collective consciousness is that you need something or someone to show up in some particular way in order to tap into and stay connected to spiritual energy and your higher potential as a human being.

There is some kind of bizarre collective belief that things need to be different than how they are right now for you to experience true connection with yourself and others and for you to have an extraordinary day that makes you feel like you are living an extraordinary life.

We have all at one point or another been somewhat present for whatever is happening but are simultaneously thinking about what great future experience is coming up, and we fail to receive the once in a lifetime gift that is being given to us in the present moment.

Perhaps you have been taught or believe that to grow, evolve and be a positive person in the world, you need to go to a church, a synagogue, a temple, a sacred place, you need a priest or a rabbi or a minister, you need to do a ceremony or go on a Vision Quest to receive an empowerment or to be baptized or initiated.

All of these ways of staying connected to your essence are beautiful, helpful and supportive.

In fact, in some way, shape or form I offer many of these things to those I love, support and serve.

However, if you start to create a mind-set that you need specific people, places and things to show up in a specific way in order to tap into your highest potential as a spiritual human being, then you will miss out on the everyday magic that is right here, right now, wherever you are.

As Mary Oliver said,

"You don't have to walk on your knees for a hundred miles through the desert repenting (in order to be a good person or have a profound spiritual experience)."

As you have noticed, the world is rapidly changing.

It used to be that we had to physically go, or sometimes walk on our knees repenting on our way, to a specific place with a specific person, such as a church or a ceremony, in order to go through a spiritual initiation or have a spiritual experience.

Nowadays, you can join a Live Stream and be a part of a church service or go through a sacred ceremony or be a part of a powerful ritual online from the comfort of your own home.

It is amazing and an incredible way to tap into powerfully supportive energy that you wouldn't otherwise be able to access if it weren't for the internet.

But sometimes you just want a real connection with a real Person, in person, who is right in front of you.

You want to make eye contact with people, shake hands with them, give them a hug and have a face-to-face conversation with them.

After all, connection with your truest, deepest and highest self and connection with other wonderful people, places and things is what makes you feel like life is amazing.

Remember that studies show that, at the end of your life, it will most likely be the relationships that you cultivated in your life that will make you feel like you had a successful and fulfilling life.

In order to feel connected, you need to connect.

That's right.

YOU.

Sometimes we push that responsibility off onto other people.

We think that another person should be the kind one, the brave one, the one that creates the connection and makes something special.

But you are the one who can create connected, magical, spiritually uplifting and beautiful interactions everywhere you go.

I know you connect with the people you already know: your friends, family, community and those you work with.

But there are also fulfilling connections available everywhere, every place with everyone all the time.

Every moment of your life can be a moment of connection and it doesn't require any special circumstances for you to experience connection.

In this way, every moment, every situation and every person can be a part of the daily adventure, Vision quest, spiritual ceremony, powerful ritual, transformational initiation and uplifting church service of your beautiful life.

The world is your temple and it is filled with wise ones, extraordinary human beings and incredible spiritual energy.

One of my favorite sayings is,

If anything is sacred, then everything is sacred.

Or

If anything is spiritual, then everything is spiritual.

Everything that happens to you is an opportunity for you to grow and evolve as a human being and a spiritual being.

Every moment is a moment when you can give and receive positive, life-affirming energy.

The trick to experiencing the profound power and connection that is always available to you is to focus on what you have and what is already here, not on what you don't have.

Be truly present right here and right now with whomever is right here and now and be truly grateful for everyone and everything in your presence.

That is the key to connection.

That is what makes every moment and every interaction an initiation.

You see, whatever is happening right now is your initiation into being the best you that you can possibly be.

I have traveled all over the world.

I have visited so many temples, churches and sacred places.

I have been with Enlightened Masters and Illuminated Souls.

I have received Spiritual Empowerments and have been initiated into different Spiritual traditions.

I used to think I had to go and do something way outside the box or travel halfway across the world or take a workshop with a spiritual teacher to have profound experiences.

I still absolutely love visiting sacred sites and visiting special places, but I recognize now that every place I am is sacred, spiritual and special.

And everyone in my presence is an expression of God/ Creator/Great Spirit/or whatever one calls the Great Mystery.

More and more as I connect with and stay aligned with my truest, deepest and highest Self and stay connected to my Purpose, Values, Message and Vision, I find that every day in so many ways I have profound interactions and connections . . . oftentimes with perfect strangers that I may never see again.

As Maya Angelou said,

"People don't remember what you say or do, people remember how they felt in your presence."

You showing up as your best self at the grocery store, at the restaurant, on your walk or anywhere else you happen to be in the world is what you can do right now to positively change this world. Just your normal everyday interactions with people as you journey through your day can make every day feel special for you and everyone you encounter.

When I say hello or wave to someone on the street, friends will often ask me,

"Do you know that person?"

I always say,

"I do now."

No one is a stranger.

Everyone can be your friend, teacher and student.

One of my favorite quotes by an unknown author is,

Love makes the Soul come out of its hiding place.

Flowing love can be very simple. Simply,

Smile.

Say hello.

Ask: How are you today?

Give a simple compliment.

Open the door for someone.

Say something offbeat and funny.

Be open to whomever and whatever is right here right now.

This moment.

This person.

This place.

This thing.

This is the ceremony.

This is the adventure.

This is the playground.

This is the initiation.

Your future is not being created in the future.

Your future is being created right now by how you are showing up right now.

Everyone and everything you have been looking for is right here right now or will somehow lead you to the right person, place and thing.

But you have to be fully present right now with whomever is here right now in order to be led to and to be able to connect with your most fulfilling relationships and connections.

You have to be fully present with whatever is happening right now in order to be led to and to be able to access your most fulfilling future.

The bible says,

The Kingdom of Heaven is within.

Heaven is right here and right now.

If you don't care to get Biblical about it, then take a hint from one of pop culture's beloved songwriters Belinda Carlisle who said,

"Heaven is a place on Earth. They say in Heaven love comes first. We'll make Heaven a place on Earth."

So don't put off heavenly true connections until later.

When you are fully present and cultivate the perspective that you are in the right place at the right time, and that this is Heaven, it's possible to feel like every day you are in a sacred place, on a Vision quest connecting with magical beings.

My feeling is that so many of us have underestimated how important we are and what a huge and positive difference we can make in the world.

My intention is to inspire you to go out and co-create beautiful interactions with the people, places and things that you encounter every day more and more.

I have put together a collection of true life stories that happened to me. They are here to inspire you, to uplift you and to give you a daily dose of real connection and true fulfillment.

While writing this very chapter, a man approached me as I was working away on my Apple computer. He asked,

"Is it true? Does an Apple a day keep the doctor away?"

I said,

"If you are doing what I am doing with the Apple, then yes indeed, an Apple a day will keep the doctor away."

He said,

"Well, what are you doing with that Apple?"

I said,

"I am writing."

He said,

"What are you writing?"

I said,

"I am writing a book about transforming the world and truly loving every day of your life by being a benevolent force of goodness with everyone and everything everywhere."

And with a sparkle in his eyes he said,

"Congratulations . . . that is a very good way to keep the doctor away."

And just like that, he and I became the main characters in the sweet and meaningful short story that we co-created together.

We initiated each other into deeper connection with each other simply by being truly present with each other . . . and we were both smiling ear to ear after our brief interaction.

It made my night and I have a feeling it made his night too.

You are the main character and Director in your stories.

The more that you take responsibility for creating magic in your own life with everyone you meet, the more you will feel like every moment is a special and sacred story that you are blessed to be in.

AA Malee said,

"Ah, kindness. What a simple way to tell another struggling Soul that there is love to be found in this world."

It all begins with basic kindness.

Even when you're not feeling your 100 percent best.

Simply cultivating, giving and sharing basic kindness with everyone and everything in your presence . . . including you . . . will always make you feel like you are part of the force of goodness that is ever expanding in the world.

Right here.

Right now.

I love you and I support you.

THE INITIATION

Many people are going through massive initiations initiated by Mother Nature right now: Fires, Earthquakes and Hurricanes are happening all over our planet right now and I have gone through some huge initiations initiated by Mother Nature too.

While on an extraordinary trip to the Kootenays in British Columbia, Canada, I was beyond awe inspired by Mother Earth and the natural world.

While in Canada I was traveling with four dear hearts nearly three hours away from our home base to go on a hike, high up into the Alpines.

Just the day before, I went on an epic hike through a gorgeous forest around a giant lake with my two incredible friends who were hosting me at their Shangri-La.

It was typical Fall weather, a little chilly, but nice.

I wore several layers and my very thin Vibram Five Finger shoes.

By thin I mean a quarter-inch total including the rubber sole and the inner foot pad.

I love wearing my Vibram Five Fingers because I can really feel and connect with the Earth when I walk.

It's the closest thing I have ever experienced to being barefoot.

We all assumed that the weather and conditions would be more or less the same as they were the day before.

As we drove higher and higher into the mountains, snow began to fall.

It was so lovely.

By the time we reached the parking lot at the base of the Monica Meadows trail, we were surrounded by a lot of ground snow and snow-covered trees and it was snowing.

The trail was more or less straight up.

At first the trail was mostly dirt with snow on the edges, but within ten minutes the entire trail was pure snow, it was snowing even more and we were surrounded by even more snow-covered trees.

IT WAS GLORIOUSLY BEAUTIFUL.

AND . . .

I was walking on snow for what would turn out to be three hours.

AND . . .

My feet were friggin' freezing.

So,

My choices were:

Turn around and wait in the car for several hours and miss out on the hike and what would turn out to be some of the most extraordinary natural beauty I have ever seen . . .

OR . . .

Put into practice every major Jedi mind trick, Yogi superpower, mind over matter, I am in control of my body practice I have ever practiced.

Every day I practice.

I condition my body, mind, heart, Soul and Spirit to work together as a team so that I can tap into my highest potential as consistently as I can so that I love my life and feel aligned with my truest, deepest and highest Self while being of the greatest service possible in the world.

And THIS was the advanced course for me.

THIS is where the rubber meets the road . . . or in this case where my nearly bare feet meet the snow.

On my drive from Spokane, Washington, to Canada I listened to *The War of Art* by Steven Pressfield.

It really inspired me and it totally kicked my ass.

I started hearing his wise teachings as I walked up the mountain. Especially the part about resistance.

"The more important a call or action is to our Soul's evolution, the more resistance we will feel toward pursuing it."

Damn.

I was feeling resistant to the call.

This was Canada's initiation for me and I had to decide if I was going to hike up the proverbial mountain or, well, you know, quit.

Of course 10,000 thoughts passed through my mind:

You're crazy.

This is insane.

What the heck are you doing?

Turn back.

Play it safe.

And, of course, *How the heck am I going to do this?*

I checked in with my inner team.

Mind, Heart, Soul and Spirit were onboard saying,

"WE CAN DO THIS!

IT'S GOING TO BE INCREDIBLE!

LOOK AT HOW INCREDIBLY BEAUTIFUL IT IS!"

My body was the resistant one saying,

"Ummmm . . .

What about me?

It's my feet that that have to do this and I am afraid of:

Frostbite

Losing my toes

Slipping

Falling down the mountain

Twisting my ankles

Twisting my knees

Cracking my head open."

My four compadres were a blend of Yogis, Meditators, Life Coaches, High Human Potential students and practitioners, Nature lovers and incredibly loving and supportive.

One of my new friends had been a lead nature adventure guide for a wide range of individuals, nonprofits and corporate partners and has taken hundreds of groups into the wilderness for life-changing and community building experiences.

Oh, and there was this one very cute dog with us who was barefoot. He didn't even have quarter-inch soled Vibram Five Fingers on.

So I was in very good company and really wanted to experience this epic adventure with all of them.

The dog became my partner in snow walking.

If he can do it, I can do it.

So, I made a decision.

I committed.

I stepped into that experience, into that challenge, into the cold, and into the freeze with 100 percent of my body, mind, heart, Soul and Spirit.

And when I stepped in fully I was not doing it alone.

Not only were my four human friends and dog friend with me, I also felt the presence of:

My guides and guardians, the indwelling teacher within my heart and every powerful and positive teacher I have ever encountered in this lifetime and beyond, the most benevolent Gods and Goddesses, Angels and Archangels, the ascended, illuminated, enlightened Masters, my truest, deepest and highest Self, my future Self having successfully and healthfully accomplished my mission and vision, all of Nature and the Nature Spirits, the sky, sun, moon, stars and planets, the Earth, land, water (including the snow), animals, plants and minerals, the elementals earth, water, fire, air, space, light and the celestial cosmos, the four sacred directions north, south, east and west, and my seven energy centers, my Chakras.

I always connect with them and call upon them several times a day and have a deep, current, powerful relationship with them all that I constantly cultivate so I knew they were already with me, loving and supporting me every freezing step of the way.

I asked them as I always do to please lead me, guide me, direct me and protect me in my thoughts, feelings, words, deeds and in all of my relationships with all people, places and things on all levels, planes and dimensions of reality in the seen and the unseen realms during this experience as I always ask them to do every moment of my life.

And . . .

I felt the presence and activation of every spiritual teaching that I have ever learned and practiced.

I deeply felt the presence of a former partner who I went on many outdoor adventures with, including attending Tom Brown's Outdoor Survival School for a week of camping off-grid in the Pine Barrens forest in New Jersey.

Tom Brown is an outdoor survival guide and teacher whose teachings and presence have had a huge positive influence on me and my life.

He has written several books.

The first one I read is The Quest and it was a gift from my former partner.

In it Tom tells the story of his teacher whose name was Grandfather. Grandfather initiated many initiations for Tom, including jumping into and sitting for long periods of time in nearly frozen ponds and lakes.

He would have to activate his inner fire to keep his body warm or else he would freeze to death.

He had to practice mind over matter and spirit over body.

He had to commune with nature always rather than resist it.

I had to practice those very things.

I have a powerful relationship with the element fire so I called upon Agni, the Sanskrit name for fire and the God of Fire.

I visualized that my feet were hot and were melting steady stable grooves into the snow so that I would be simultaneously warm and sure-footed.

I prayed.

I chanted.

I invoked.

I visualized.

I was present.

I was focused.

I was meditating while in motion.

I went into a total flow state.

Every person that passed me by said something akin to,

"Are you okay walking in those shoes? That must be gnarly."

Someone said,

"I am worried about your feet."

I responded,

"Please don't project anything negative onto my feet.

Please visualize them warm, stable and healthy. Thank you."

It didn't help when we saw a bunch of blood splattered on the trail.

Shit.

That made my mind wobble.

I had a few flashes of me slipping, falling and cracking my head open.

Which of course made me feel slippy.

No Anne!

No!

You can't afford to wobble for even a moment.

You are way the heck out here now and you are not going to get airlifted out of here if you slip and fall if you start focusing on what you DON'T want to have happen.

So . . .

BE HERE NOW.

OKAY, OKAY I AM HERE.

More prayers + More chants + More invocations + More positive visualizations of what I want + More presence + More focus + More meditation in motion = Deep flow state.

Along the way, the most beautiful Winter Wonderland ever.

One of those is-this-really-happening?! environments.

I felt like I had walked through the magical closet in *The Chronicles of Narnia* and ended up in the realm of snow-covered magic making.

Oh yeah, and the day before I acquired a handcrafted custom broom from a magical White Wizard named Luke (and THE FORCE is definitely with him) who custom created all the brooms for Harry Potter and Bewitched so I visualized that I was riding my broom too. And then . . .

We arrived at our destination, Monica's Meadow.

It was nothing short of spectacular.

We all gazed in awe.

Everyone was just standing there awestruck.

That wasn't an option for me.

Had I done that the freeze would have taken over my feet.

So I danced.

I flash danced.

And of course I sang:

"Like a maniac

A maniac on the snow

And she's dancin' like she's never danced before . . ."

I had to for survival . . .

I practice that dance a lot too.

It's a normal part of my repertoire.

So it was right there for me to tap into when I really needed it.

THE POWER OF PRACTICE PROVED ITSELF TO ME yet again. . . .

One of my mentors Bo Eason says,

"WHAT SEPARATES THE AMATEUR FROM THE PRO IS THEIR RELATIONSHIP TO PRACTICE."

And then there is good ole:

Luck is when preparation meets opportunity.

Daily practice and preparation is where it's at.

When the shit hits the fan and I have to master the moment and whatever the moment brings, my daily health and wellness practices get me through.

And during that moment I had to pull out the big guns.

The sunlight was slowly starting to fade.

It was getting colder.

The trail was getting a lot more slippery.

My hands were now starting to freeze.

One of my dear hearts gave me one of her gloves.

Then she gave me the other one.

She really was my Angel in that moment and I will never forget her selfless generosity.

It was a lot colder and a lot more slippery on the way down the mountain.

I started chanting to Ganesha, the Hindu God that removes obstacles.

OM GAM GANAPATAYE NAMAHA

Over and over and over . . .

Out loud . . .

I later learned that one of my new friends asked another one of our friends, "What is that low guttural sound?"

My other friend replied, "Oh, that's Anne chanting to Ganesha."

Then I started praying out loud to Mother Earth and to the snow,

"I am humble.

I am your humble child.

I am here to completely merge with you.

I am here to totally harmonize with you.

I honor you.

I bless you.

You are my Mama.

You are so powerful.

I know you can flick me off this mountain or freeze me at any moment and I am so grateful for your love and support.

I love you and I support you.

I am breathing out so that you can survive.

I am breathing in so that I can survive.

I know we are in this together.

Thank you.

Thank you.

Thank you."

And I felt her holding me.

I felt the reciprocity.

I felt our connection.

I felt the harmony.

I felt like I was truly in the right relationship with her more than I have ever been in my entire life.

It's like that with all of our relationships.

As humans, we have to talk with each other to feel that connection. It's one of the five Love Languages.

Just thinking about someone or texting them or sending photos or doing nothing is not enough to keep a relationship thriving. We need sound vibration.

We need to hear our own voice.

We need to hear the voice of our Beloveds.

It creates trust.

It creates an environment of love, communion, presence, power, passion and connection.

This is what the word ABRACADABRA means:

I speak it and SO IT IS.

So I spoke to Mother Earth and my guides and teachers and my Higher Self the entire way down that mountain.

I couldn't afford to drop the ball and get lazy for even a second.

I needed to continuously cultivate my connection to all of the seen and unseen love and support in existence without wavering so that it was clearly seen, felt, heard and known that I deeply care and am deeply devoted to my life and am living a supercharged life.

I needed to remind myself and all of existence that I AM IN.

And this is what happened:

Not only did I feel myself in a pretty much perpetual flow state,

I WAS IN BLISS.

What I realized and remembered was,

It doesn't matter what situation I am in, be it super challenging or super easy . . . When I am 100 percent present, I tap into a deep sense of true happiness and fulfillment.

And my big takeaway was,

What would my life be like if I was this way in every moment with every experience, person, place and thing?

What would my life be like if I stopped dispersing my precious life force energy and stopped giving myself 100 percent to experiences, people, places and things that don't give their 100 percent to me?

What would my life be like if I stopped leaking my physical, mental, emotional, spiritual and soul energy to anything that is not aligned with what I actually want to create in my life?

What would my life be like if I only flowed my mojo to experiences, people, places and things where I AM IN 100 percent?

My life would truly feel like a benevolent extension and expression of Great Spirit's grace.

I feel this a lot in my life . . .

AND I am devoted to up-leveling and deepening this way of being because it truly is fulfilling for me and I feel it is a core key for me to be of greater service on our beautiful planet.

When we reached the end of the hike and stepped off the trail, I wondered how my feet would be.

Much to my surprise my feet were not frozen and in no time they were warm and cozy.

Thank goodness I prepared ahead of time for that very moment:

My furry booties were waiting for me in the car.

My new friend who is an outdoor adventure and nature guide told me that he had never seen someone do what I did and that it was equivalent to walking on hot coals for three hours like Tony Robbins does as the final initiation with his students.

I told all my friends that I could not have done it without them.

I truly felt like they had my back the entire time.

I felt so much love and support from them all and I will always feel a very special bond with them.

They were joking around and calling me FRO-TOE or "She who walks with frozen feet."

It was hilarious. . . .

AND I claimed for myself that I actually wasn't lil Ms. Frozen Toes because I overcame the cold.

So they now call me:

She who walks with hot feet

Or simply,

Hot Feet.

It certainly was an initiation for me and I am changed forever.

It was like a mini near-death experience for me.

I feel deeply humbled and grateful.

Life feels even more precious to me.

My love, time and energy feels more precious to me.

AND

It has become crystal clear when I am in the presence of people, places and things who are navigating life in this way.

That's the energy that I consciously choose to be around.

As I reflect on the word initiation I see that the first four letters spell IN IT.

The purpose of any initiation is to initiate us into being fully IN IT.

IN IT with life.

IN IT with ourselves.

IN IT with our relationships with people, places and things.

Being all the way IN IT is true INtimacy.

If we are not going to be totally 100 percent IN IT with anything, then what is the point?

Really.

Truly.

One of my favorite sayings is

99 percent is a bitch. 100 percent is a breeze.

The question that I brought down from the mountain for us all and life's question for us all every day is:

ARE YOU IN?

I AM.

I NEED LOVE

One morning I was having breakfast in the main lodge at the Esalen Institute in Big Sur, California, where I was teaching Yoga, Breathwork, Meditation and a workshop about the Chakras.

A wonderful woman at our table asked me if I was going to the Million Women March in Washington, DC in January.

I told her that I was open to it but have no plans to go at this moment and that I am doing my best to think nationally and globally but am consciously choosing to act locally by embodying the love, grace, power, dignity and goodness of all womankind by being truly present and loving with each and every person in my presence right now every day.

Within an hour I was walking through the lodge and a couple stopped me and the gentleman said,

"Excuse me. Do you have a moment?"

I replied,

"Yes."

He proceeded by saying,

"We were just observing the many people here and were pondering who is the most profound person here this weekend. My feeling is that it is you."

I smiled and responded,
"Well, thank you Sir. I feel honored that you see me this way."

He smiled and continued,
"My question for you is, what is the most profound bit of wisdom that you have for me?"

She said while giggling,
"No pressure. He just sees you as the most profound person here who has the most profound wisdom in all of existence."

I giggled.

And then I paused for a moment as I realized THIS is one of those profound moments when I have the opportunity to make a profound impact in the most positive way possible in this once in a lifetime never to happen again moment.

And . . . I have practiced for this moment.

And . . . I AM READY.

I looked him in the eyes and said,
"What do you need more than anything right now?"

He said,
"Well, what do any of us need right now?"

I said,

"That's another question."

Then with even deeper presence and a bit more intense warmth in my eyes and voice as if I turned up the fire of presence within me, I asked,

"What do YOU need right now?"

He replied,

"Well, I NEED LOVE."

I smiled my biggest and warmest smile, leaned down on bended knee in the spirit of great devotion, took his hands in my hands, looked deeply into his eyes and said, "I love you. On behalf of myself, all of humanity and all of existence, I am sorry for anything that I, anyone or anything that exists has ever thought, felt, said or done that in any way has caused you harm or made you doubt the inherent goodness of life. Please forgive me. Please forgive us all. You matter. You make a difference. You are very important. Thank you for existing. Thank you for being here. I am grateful for you."

As I spoke, tears welled up in and then fell from his blue eyes.

He said,

"That is the most profound thing anyone has ever said to me. Thank you. I love you."

We hugged and told each other again,

"I love you."

I looked at her and said,

"I love you too."

She said,

"I love you too."

She said,

"Well, I guess he was right. When he told me he thought you are the most profound person here I told him, 'She just might be the most profound person here. And, she just might be from Argentina.'"

I was wearing black jeans, a black-button down shirt, a black cape, a black Stetson hat and black shitkicker cowgirl boots.

I guess I looked like an Argentinian cowgirl.

So of course I laughed and did my best tango that I could possibly conjure up and did my special wild pony dance . . . as one does in moments like this.

And then I said,

"I now understand the word profound in a way I never have before. The word PRO means being the best that you can be.

The word FOUND means finding something.

Maybe being profound is about finding those amazing and best parts of ourselves, others and life that we lost touch with or forgot about somewhere along the way and bringing them back to life.

Maybe it's about finding and discovering the best parts of ourselves, others and all of life that have been here all along that we never knew existed."

Today, as always, being truly profound is about being human. Being: A human who cares. A human who loves. A human who knows, remembers and reminds everyone in her presence that we are all connected and we all matter.

As I walked away from that kind couple who saw the best in me and asked me one of the most powerful questions I have ever been asked, I realized that I am already on the Million Women's March.

I am marching with every man, woman, child and living being who decides in every moment with every person, place and thing to
CHOOSE LOVE AND BE KIND.

Thank you for marching, dancing and loving with me.

THIS IS OUR COVENANT

I have had the great honor of telling the story of my Dad's passing and all of the life after death experiences that I have had with him many times since 1998 when he passed from this world to the next.

I have a dear friend named William Peters who founded the Shared Crossing Project whose mission is to raise awareness and educate people about the profound and healing experiences that are available for the dying and their loved ones at the end of life.

You can visit sharedcrossing.com to learn more.

William asked me to write the story, share it with the members of the Shared Crossing Project and asked to include it in his research project.

It was a cathartic experience for me to write this story and to share it.

My relationship with my father, who passed in 1998, is just as powerful now as it was when he was on planet Earth and our love and connection continues to grow, prosper and evolve every day.

My Father, Eric Randolph Van de Water, was one of the most amazing humans I have ever known.

When he walked into a room everyone turned to look at him.

He had a light and smile that illuminated the world.

He had an unforgettable presence.

He had a lot of spirit but didn't consider himself to be spiritual.

If anything, nature was his church and in nature he connected with the Great Mystery.

When I was fourteen, I took a class at Santa Barbara High School called Language in Human Relationships and was asked some deep and profound questions about life and living.

When I was asked "How is your relationship with your parents?" I realized that I could either have two best friends or two worst enemies and I would much rather have two best friends.

From that moment forward I was a loyal best friend to my dear ole dad and to this day, my Mom is one of best friends in the world.

When my Father was diagnosed with esophageal cancer, he was fifty-five and I was twenty-seven.

At the time I was in India traveling with a spiritual teacher and was teaching Yoga at her retreats.

On the eleventh day of what can only be described as a Samadhi Enlightenment experience, I called home like I did every week to connect with my family and sadly learned that my dad had been diagnosed with esophageal cancer.

The Doctor, who was apparently void of all compassion and empathy, sat back in his chair, kicked his feet up on the desk, crisscrossed his feet, looked my Dad in the eyes and said, "Well Eric, you're going to die."

Later that day, at sunset, an owl flew just one inch above my dad's head and called out three times.

Some Native American tribes believe that when the owl calls your name, you will soon be leaving this world.

My dad was fit as a fiddle, handsome, active and looked like he was in perfect health, so it was a huge shock to us all.

I wanted to go home right away to be with him but he said, "No, I need you to stay there with your enlightened ones and pray for me," which was highly uncharacteristic of him.

I later learned that he had recently read *The Tibetan Book of Living and Dying.*

I stayed in India for another month and sent him faxes and letters and called often with messages that gave very clear support and hot tips on how to navigate the cancer storm physically, emotionally, mentally and spiritually.

During that remaining month in India I had profoundly challenging experiences of facing my own death and mortality as a human being and profoundly enlightening experiences of recognizing that as a spiritual being I will never die and am immortal.

He lived for a total of nine months after he was diagnosed.

It took him nine months to prepare for this world in his mother's womb. It took him nine months to prepare to leave this world.

During the nine-month transition he had chemo and radiation and had his esophagus removed.

It was one of the most challenging things I have ever experienced — watching the superman who could do just about anything lose 25 percent of his original 200 lbs and not be able to do all of the vital physical activity that was his daily norm.

The most challenging part was to witness his psycho-emotional struggles.

At night he couldn't sleep because he was so concerned about leaving us and leaving my mom with the burden of so much to take care of in the material world.

He was deeply stressed.

Stress wasn't new to him.

In fact it contributed to his cancer, but this was a different kind of stress.

It was the stress that a dying person who had not cultivated a deep daily relationship with his non physical/mental/ emotional self goes through while trying to transition from the material world to the spiritual world.

At night he wanted to be tucked in . . . it was really sweet.

It was like a role reversal, where I, the child, became the parent to my parent.

Sometimes he would call to me when he couldn't sleep.

I would get in bed with him and hold his hand and lead him on guided meditations.

We both loved the ocean and went scuba diving and swam with wild dolphins together.

So in the meditations I would ask him to visualize that the stress he was feeling was choppy water at the surface of the sea.

I told him that in the same way that when we scuba dive we were able to go beneath the choppy water at the surface of the sea and go down into the deep stillness and peace of the sea, we can do the same thing mentally and emotionally.

I would then guide him beneath the stressful surface of his thoughts and emotions to the deep stillness and peace of his innermost being and spirit.

He would always fall asleep during the meditation and sleep through the night.

During those meditations he shared that he began to connect with who he is beyond his body, mind and heart.

As his life force dwindled away we started to talk about the time when Hospice would come.

He would always say that as soon as Hospice came, it would be his cue to pass away because it would mean that taking care of him had become too much of a burden for us.

In the months leading up to his death, he would have dreams and visions of the other side.

He owned a boat and a Suburban and an Airstream trailer and when he would tune into wherever it was that he was going after this life, he would say, "There is no space for me there. And there is no space for my boat, Suburban and Airstream."

That really stressed him out because he felt trapped between two worlds. From there on out I would lead him on guided meditations where he was traveling along a road in his Suburban towing his Airstream and boat.

I would have him visualize that he was traveling to a specific destination and that he would pull into a big parking lot where there were three available parking spots, one for his Suburban, one for his boat and one for his Airstream.

Within a couple of weeks, late at night, during a vision, on his own accord, he said,

"They made a space for me."

It was then that I knew he was going to be okay and that he would soon be transitioning.

A week before he passed, my friend who was the spiritual teacher that I had been traveling with in India said,

"Your father is going to pass soon and you need to clear some things with him."

I knew exactly what she was talking about and went directly to my parent's house and asked my dad if I could talk with him.

He agreed.

I told him that I had very challenging things to express to him that I had been holding in my heart for my whole life.

I asked him if it was okay to share some things that might be challenging and upsetting for him to hear.

He agreed.

For the next fifteen minutes I told him about every time he disappointed and let me down as a father and a friend.

I told him about every pain, upset, resentment, sadness and disappointment that I had ever experienced in my relationship with him.

It was the most challenging, cathartic and brave thing that I had ever done with him.

I uncontrollably sobbed the entire time.

When I finished I simply said,

"That's it."

He simply responded,

"Will you forgive me?"

I said,

"Yes. Will you forgive me for carrying these grudges for all these years?"

He said,

"Yes. You don't know how much this helps me to let go. Thank you."

We hugged and told each other that we loved each other.

The next day Hospice came to talk to us about what would happen when we requested Hospice care for my dad.

We all sat in the living room and talked about the details.

It was during that conversation that I looked at my dad and said, "After you pass away, will you please let us know that you safely made it to wherever you are going?"

He said,

"Yes I will."

The next day he told me that I was on the right path and that if he had to live this life all over again that he would choose to walk the path that I am on.

51

Within days he was definitely preparing to leave this life.

I stayed with him for three days straight.

I didn't leave the house at all.

On the third night my mom called my boyfriend at the time and asked him to please come and take me out on a date because I had not left the house in three days.

When he came to get me, I went into the bedroom where my dad was fast asleep.

I went over to him, kissed him on the cheek and whispered in his ear, "I love you."

As I walked away, he said,

"I love you Annie girl."

Those were our last words.

That night Hospice came.

He passed away the next morning at dawn.

He told us that the moment that Hospice came would be the moment that he would know that it was time for him to go.

He kept his word, just like he said he would.

Just like he always did.

Later that day my sister and I went out to go to the grocery store. When we were driving down our little lane I spotted what I thought was a rat or a mouse in the middle of the road.

I said,

"Stop the car. There's a critter in the road."

I got out of the car and walked over to what turned out to be a cockatiel bird.

I leaned down to see if it was okay and it hopped right over to me and up onto my hand.

He then walked up my arm, sat on my shoulder and started to make gentle chirping sounds in my ear while preening my hair.

And he wouldn't leave.

So we got in the car with him chirping and preening me and drove the rest of the way down the lane to my family's home.

As we drove along I realized that my dad had made his safe passage from this world to the next.

Birds are messengers from the spirit world.

Once again, my dad kept his word and had sent me a sign that he was okay.

This wondrous bird wanted to stay with us so we took him inside.

It was sunset.

I had decided that for the first three nights after my dad's passing that I was going to do rituals and ceremonies to help his soul get to wherever it was going. Even though he had given me the very clear sign that he made it to his next destination, I still wanted to do the rituals and ceremonies to honor him.

I put the cockatiel on the edge of a chair, started lighting candles, chanting and doing my rituals for my dad.

At one point I was drawn to a flickering shadow that I saw on the wall behind the bird.

There was a candle that was shining light on the profile of the bird's face and reflecting his silhouette onto the wall.

In college my dad's buddies called him "The Buzzard" because he had a prominent bird-like beak of a nose.

When I looked over, what I saw, was the perfect silhouette of my father's face.

That bird wasn't only a messenger on my dad's behalf.

He was my dad, or at least a fragment of my dad's Soul was imprinted in the bird.

So my sister kept him as a pet and we named him Skeeder, which was one of my dad's nicknames derived from one of our secret languages.

A week later at my dad's memorial service about six hundred people showed up at the Natural History Museum to honor him.

I had written a song called "From God Knows Where" that I sang for him at the Memorial Service.

I sang the first two verses:

It's a moonless night, but the stars they do shine bright.

No matter how dark it becomes, the light shall prevail.

So dance with the darkness.

Become one with the mystery.

Look your shadow in the eye and see the Truth is . . .

Here. Here. Here.

The Truth is Here.

There's a bare limbed tree, but the roots still run deep.

In the autumn breeze the leaves fall down, for they know that the sky is one with the ground.

So let your leaves go and then the secret you will know.

Only when you release do you realize you are already . . .

Free. Free. Free.

You are already Free.

While I sang that verse a wind picked up and I felt my dad's spirit with absolute certainty.

And he began to give me a fourth verse to the song.

It was one of the most bizarre and incredible musical experiences of my life. While singing I realized that the song was about how my dad passed from this world to the next.

And it was quite a process to sing the third verse while receiving and downloading a fourth verse from my dad who had showed up as the wind. Especially in front of six hundred people at my dad's memorial service.

The third verse is:

And it's a stormy sea, but beneath stillness and peace.

The waves will always rise and fall, but the silent deep will remain.

So dive into the ocean.

Allow yourself to flow with the come 'n' go.

Feel the crashing upon the shore and know, you're always . . .

Home. Home. Home.

You're always Home.

It was the meditation I had guided him through so many times.

And then the fourth verse came through for the first time ever:

And the one you love is gone but will never really die.

For there is no death, just a change of worlds.

He is the wave flowing.

He is the tree.

He is the breeze blowing.

He is free. He is free. He is free.

This man who was my father who I didn't think was very spiritual ended up being a true enlightened master who truly got this whole amazing mysterious existence by consciously dying and allowing me to be with him on every level, plane and dimension of reality.

A week later in the middle of the night, the phone rang and I picked it up.

This was not a dream.

I was definitely awake.

It was my dad.

He said,

"Hello my precious gem."

That's what he always called me because we were both Geminis and gem was a double entendre for being a Gemini and his precious jewel.

I was speechless and he knew it.

He said,

"It's okay, Annie."

Once I could speak I said,

"How are you?"

He said,

"All is well. I am just so sorry that I had to leave you, mom and your sister."

I said,

"Where are you?"

He said,

"I am HERE now."

I knew that he had merged with the eternal NOW that connects the past, present and future.

I asked,

"Why did you have to go?"

He said,

"I was called here to help others go through the same process that I just went through. Thank you for your help. There are many that are passing over now and need my help to go through what you helped me go through."

I told him,

"I love you."

He said,

"I love you and I will always be with you."

And he has kept his word to me.

I feel him with me always.

He is one of my best friends and Guardian Angels.

Any time I really need him and call for him, he comes.

After he passed away, my mom gave me his Acura Legend.

I really loved that car.

One time I was driving it along a windy road on a cliff and I swerved to miss a squirrel.

My car spun out of control.

I said out loud,

"I am not in control but you are, God, and I surrender."

I took my hands off the wheel, closed my eyes, called upon my dad and awaited my destiny.

The car went off the cliff and I tumbled down thirty feet to the earth below, which just so happened to be the Tennis Club of Santa Barbara.

My car landed upside down and was totaled.

I walked out without a scratch.

The head of Emergency of our local Hospital happened to be playing tennis when the accident happened.

He, the Police Officers and the paramedics who were called just in case of internal injuries all agreed that it was a total miracle that I was alive, let alone not injured at all.

He kept his word.

He helped me.

I feel his love and support every day in every way.

Even though the body of my vehicle died in that accident, I lived.

In the same way my dad's body died, but his spirit will live on forever.

What happened after my dad's passing was only possible because of how we lived and loved each other while he was alive.

One of my core spiritual practices is called Ho'o'ponopono.

It is practiced by the Kahunas of Hawaii for peacekeeping amongst tribal and family members.

It consists of four sentences:

I love you.

I am sorry.

Please forgive me.

Thank you.

It is a clearing practice.

It clears stress, tension and heavy energy between loved ones so that love, light and peace can prevail.

I didn't learn about this practice until ten years after my dad passed, but I now realize that we were practicing Ho'o'ponopono with each other.

The last words we spoke to each other were,

"I love you."

That's what this whole wild ride comes down to.

It's all about love.

But in order for love to prevail, you have to be humble and forgiving and grateful.

You have to continuously create space in your body, mind and heart for spiritual love to fill you up and lead you, guide you, direct you and protect you.

There is a saying:

It's a good day to die.

You say it when you feel like you have done everything that you could possibly do and now you can simply let go and trust in the way that things naturally unfold.

When you practice love, forgiveness, humility and gratitude, you can truly let go because your conscience is clear and you know you have done everything you can possibly do to create peace in your life and the lives of others.

And when you do, you will find the secret key to immortality.

It's the key to peace.

If everyone could easily and effortlessly say these four sentences with sincerity in their heart, we would have universal peace on this planet. And it's the key to everlasting peace beyond this world.

My dad's famous last words to me were,

"I love you."

My famous last words to him were,

"I love you."

That's what it all comes down to.

In the end, in the beginning and every step of the way, love is the way.

Love and appreciation creates a bridge between the worlds that keeps us connected to all those that have walked the path before us. That is Eric Randolph Van de Water's legacy and I exist now to carry forth, embody and share love with everyone in my presence.

And just like my dad, in life and in death, I will keep my word.

This is our covenant.

WE LOVE YOU.

PRACTICE PRACTICE PRACTICE

One time there was a 4.3 magnitude earthquake that originated deep beneath the sea on the West Coast of the United States.

I didn't feel it and had no idea that it happened in real time.

HOWEVER, in the morning just before the earthquake occurred I had a very powerful lucid dream just after listening to fifteen minutes of body-mind-heart-soul-spirit balancing Theta Brainwave music that helps me to tap into higher consciousness and elevated states of being.

In the dream I was in a beautiful home right on the beach with a loving group of friends.

I was looking out to the sea and was watching the wave patterns like any good surfer of life always does.

I noticed that moment by moment the waves were getting bigger. They were crashing more and more powerfully on the shore and then they started rising up to all the beach houses.

I said to my friends,

"I think there was an earthquake deep beneath the sea because the waves are getting really huge."

Within a minute a huge wave crashed on our house, uprooting the foundation of the house and hurling us high up into the sky.

We went flying through the air and of course panic broke out in the flying house.

For an instant I thought

Oh shit!

But quickly realized that was not going to help at all.

But prayer will.

So I yelled out,

"OM NAMAH SHIVAYA!"

Shiva is the Hindu God of destruction.

Shiva destroys our stress, our fear, our drama and our freak-out. Life as we know it cannot exist without the destructive force. We need to destroy anything that is not aligned and in harmony with all of existence.

We need to preserve everything that is aligned and in harmony with all of existence.

We need to create things that are aligned and in harmony with all of existence.

This dance of destruction, preservation and creation is eternal here on Planet Earth and will never stop.

If you don't resonate with a Hindu God named Shiva, you can simply think of Shiva as representing the everyday, all the time force of destruction that is always operating in our lives.

So basically I yelled out,

"ALL HAIL TO THE DESTRUCTIVE FORCE OF THE UNIVERSE!"

I got humble and felt that,

Hey, clearly things are a bit chaotic right now and I am just going to get crystal clear that there is not a thing that I can do to stop this destruction because it's going down.

I am going to bow down to and become a humble servant to that force of destruction that is trying to destroy whatever it's trying to destroy.

And, I am going to surrender and not fight the destructive force because I am a tiny tiny, tiny grain of sand that can be annihilated in a hot second by the Force.

In the dream, as soon as I yelled out to Shiva, everyone got instantly still and calm.

And instead of feeling like we were being uncontrollably hurled through the sky, our pace seemed to smooth as if we were slowly floating on a magic carpet.

Then I started chanting the Gayatri Mantra, a highly revered mantra from the Rig Veda, the oldest known manuscript in existence, dedicated to Savitur, the Sun deity:

om bhūr bhuvaḥ svaḥa tát savitúr várenyaṃ bhárgo devásya dhīmahi dhíyo yó naḥ prachodayāt om shanti shanti shanti

It means:

You who are the Source of all power

Whose rays illuminate the world,

Illuminate also my heart so that it too can do Your work.

Peace Peace Peace

I was calling in the big guns for love, support and protection.

Everyone joined in, simply humming along if they didn't know the words.

Within a minute we gently touched down to Earth.

No one was hurt and the house was in perfect condition.

In my waking life, I chant these prayers every single day.

They are a core part of my life.

So when the shit hits the fan and things get a little crazy they are always here for me and I remember them.

They are here for me in dreamtime and in my waking life.

When I was hurled off a thirty-foot cliff in my car, I said these prayers as I was tumbling down the hill and walked out untouched from my completely totaled car.

When a giant fire came to my neighborhood, not once but three times, and on the second time burned up everything on my property except my home and innermost garden, I said these prayers and my home was untouched by the fire.

When I walked for three hours on snow with barely any foot protection, I said these prayers and was untouched by the freeze.

When I was on a plane that hit such massive turbulence that everyone around me was having panic attacks, I said these prayers and those close enough to hear it were calmed and as soon as we hit smooth skies they all asked me to teach them the prayers because it helped them get through calmly.

I share all of this because as we all have been feeling in one way or another, Mother Earth is talking to us loud and clear and it behooves us to listen to her.

After the earthquake happened I read a little article about it.
It said,

"Have a plan and be prepared."

Beyond the physical plans and preparations for earthquakes and other natural disasters, I feel it is wise to have a plan and be prepared spiritually, mentally and emotionally.

Our daily Sadhana, or daily spiritual practice, is one of the best daily plans to help you prepare for anything that happens to you that is beyond your control.

When things happen that are beyond your control, the tendency is to panic and freak out.

But there is another way.

We all can ask for help from the unseen realms.

I once met an Astrophysicist Yogi who told me that 99.8 percent of reality is unseen.

Within that 99.8 percent of the unseen reality there is so much love and so much support for each and every one of us no matter what we are going through.

Clearly we are loved and supported because we are being breathed and something is making our organs work . . . it truly is miraculous. But we have to cultivate our relationship with the unseen realm to tap this immeasurable love and support and protection.

When we practice Yoga, Breathwork, Meditation and Prayer, or do whatever it is that you do to tap into the Benevolent Force within you and all around you, you become friendly with the unseen realm and all of the unseen help that is always here for you.

It helps you when someone cuts you off in traffic, when your child is having a meltdown, when you don't get the deal, when what you thought would be forever ends.

Your daily spiritual practices help you when things don't work out how you planned.

And the truth is things rarely turn out exactly like we think they are going to . . .

I personally like it when things turn out better than expected. But a lot of the time things don't turn out anything like I thought they would.

That's why every day another prayer I say is,

"Let all of my dreams, wishes and intentions happen in the Divine right time and in the Divine right way."

By Divine, I mean the innate intelligence of the 99.8 percent of reality that I cannot perceive . . . unless I tap into it by practicing my daily spiritual practices, which allow me to perceive more easily. When we practice, we become a lot better prepared for whatever comes.

We are better prepared mostly because our practice makes us simultaneously humble and empowered, flexible and strong, surrendered and full of faith.

When you practice, you are much better prepared for whatever destruction, preservation and creation happens to happen.

Over time, your daily spiritual practice transforms you into a vessel through which the destructive, preserving and creative force of the Universe can flow through you and have its way with you.

In Truth, we are all an extension of the Benevolent Source, so surrendering to and being of service to the Benevolent Source is just a really good idea.

It's definitely the path of least resistance.

When you stop fighting the Benevolent Source, then the earthquake or the tidal wave or the exploding volcano or the fire or the car crash or the broken heart can be a gateway into greater connection with the Benevolent Source.

I feel this is one of the reasons that we all feel so much more connected to each other during life's disasters.

My experience over and over, time and time again is that the greater purpose of destruction is to force us to surrender to the Benevolent Source.

Without the Benevolent Source we are nothing.

With the Benevolent Source at the epicenter of our everything, we are tapped into the greatest fulfillment available to us as human and spiritual beings.

So however you do it, keep doing your spiritual practice. This stuff really works wonders when you work it.

If you ever need any help with your daily spiritual practice, I am always here for you.

May you always feel loved, supported and protected by the Benevolent Source.

I love you and I support you through the destruction, preservation and creation of it all.

THE BALI GOD DOG

Only on Bali:

I was scootering my way through some winding backroads looking for a plant based vegan restaurant called Moksa that I have never been to, while chanting to Ganesha, the remover of obstacles, to help me find it.

I had to keep stopping to look at my map.

On my last stop I felt a presence close to me and looked down and there was a dog standing by me.

He looked me in the eyes and then turned his head and nodded toward the road.

I said,

"Oh, is Moksa down there?"

He smiled and winked.

I swear.

Then he started walking down the road and I followed him on my scooter.

He kept looking back and smiling at me to make sure I was following him.

He led me right into the scooter parking area right in front of the restaurant.

He stood right by my side while I locked my scooter and took my helmet off.

I looked him in the eyes and said,

"Thanks. You're the best and I appreciate you. You are truly the epitome of Balinese. You are so loving, kind, gracious and helpful. Have a beautiful night."

He nodded his head, smiled again and cruised back down the road.

After having an epic meal, I scootered my way back down the road and lo and behold my Bali dog friend ran out from his home base with a big smile on his face to wish me well on my journey.

He is just one of the countless famous Bali dogs who opens your heart with their purity of heart and makes you feel so loved and cared for.

By the way, Moksa is a term in Buddhism, Hinduism and Jainism that refers to various forms of emancipation, liberation, release and freedom from samsāra, the cycle of death and rebirth. It is a state of self-realization, self-knowledge and enlightenment.

I love that dog spelled backward is God.

It is year of the dog and I was born during year of the dog.

Tonight a God dog took me to Moksa. . . .

If anyone can take me to Moksa, it is God cleverly disguised as a Bali dog.

WE ARE ALL EARTH ANGELS

One time while I was in Big Sur, California, teaching at the Esalen Institute, my dear friend and I went on an adventure up the coast and landed at the bar at Nepenthe where we met a lovely couple.

I started doing Gypsy card readings for everyone at the bar, which a dear friend, a third generation Gypsy taught me how to do, using playing cards.

In between readings, we were having sweet, deep and connected conversations about life and living.

We were all drinking wine and one of our conversations turned to the subject of alcohol.

We were talking about how important it is to stay clear, focused, alert, present and conscientious when we consume alcohol because, if you don't, your auric field can open up and unsavory spirits can get into your body, mind and heart.

That's why they call alcohol "spirits."

If an unsavory spirit gets into you, then you might say and do things that are not aligned with who you truly are.

One of our new friends told us that she experienced that exact thing recently at a bar.

She said that a woman there had clearly had too much to drink and started saying terrible things to her.

She had never met this woman before and had not spoken to her so she had absolutely no idea why this woman was verbally assaulting her.

She said that's not the first time that has happened to her.

She said other women throughout her life, some that she knew, some that she barely knew and some that were complete strangers have said similar rude and unkind words to her.

Please note, my new friend is someone who I consider to be universally attractive and appealing.

She has long blond hair and has some of the most sparkling clear light blue eyes that I have ever seen.

And her demeanor is truly sweet.

She reminds me of an Angel.

I said,

"That's because you are beautiful, radiant, light, cheerful, kind and gracious. Your presence made those women feel bad about themselves so rather than simply being with their own uncomfortable feelings, they attacked you. That has happened to me too and it really hurts. I am so sorry. You are so beautiful, loving, warmhearted and good-natured and you deserve to be treated with honor and respect."

She thanked me.

My friend and I continued to talk to each other and the lovely couple continued to talk to each other.

About ten minutes later, the woman got off her barstool and walked over to me.

She was crying.

She was cathartically crying. She said,

"Thank you for everything that you expressed to me.

You made sense out of something for me that has confused and hurt me for my entire life.

And the fact that the message was delivered from a beautiful, loving and gracious woman who isn't trying to take me down makes it extra special.

Thank you."

I gave her a giant hug and told her that I love her.

We have been friends ever since.

In fact, my wonderful new friends visited me after that in Santa Barbara. It was so easy and comfortable with them that it feels as if we have known each other for a long, long time.

It's like that when you have stripped down, bare to the bone, authentic heart-centered conversations with people based on a reciprocal foundation of love.

I am reflecting on what a huge impact we all have on each other and the course of each other's lives.

Everything we say to each other can take someone down or lift someone up.

One sentence can haunt someone for their entire life.

One sentence can heal a lifetime of hurt.

We are that powerful.

It's important to be awake and aware.

When someone bares their Soul to you, it's a big responsibility.

You hold their heart in your hands.

How present you are with their vulnerability and sensitivity is a precious and defining moment.

When someone shows you their heart and Soul, show yours to them. This is how friendship, intimacy, trust and love is created.

As an unknown wise one once said,

"Love takes an act of courage and an act of surrender."

And women, please, let's all continue to love, support, respect, honor, cherish, adore and compliment each other.

Let's lift each other up and celebrate our collective beauty, compassion, gratitude, kindness and goodness.

We are all Earth Angels.

Let's continue to remind each other how wondrous, unique and special we all are.

HONORING WOMEN AS AN HONORABLE WOMAN

On honoring women and being an honorable woman.

Since 2000 I have taught Yoga at the Cancer Center of Santa Barbara.

During that time for two years I taught my classes at a temporary location where I became friends with the sweet guys that parked my car.

Every time I arrived and left, if they did not have people waiting for or needing help, we would always chat, joke around, give each other hugs and tell each other that we appreciate each other.

They called me "Yogita" . . . it was pretty cute.

One day a new guy started working as a car parker.

He was a really nice, respectful and kind man.

When he started, the other car parkers told me not to hug him because his wife didn't want him hugging other women.

At first I was surprised because I am an honorable woman and my hugs for any man other than my partner always come from a place of Universal Love and care without any sexual or romantic energy infused into them.

Just beyond that first moment of surprise, though, I immediately thought of his wife and her feelings and her request.

Because I honor women, I didn't think another moment about why she didn't want her husband to hug me or any other woman.

Why she doesn't want women hugging her husband doesn't matter. What matters is that I as a woman honor another woman and her wishes with regard to her husband, partner or lover.

Maybe she is feeling insecure, jealous, possessive, suspicious or is feeling low self-esteem.

Maybe she is working on building trust and confidence.

Maybe she is simply wanting to create a safe and sacred container with her husband.

I have felt those things too to greater or lesser degrees.

There is not one woman on the planet that I have ever met who hasn't felt those feelings too.

It's not my place to judge her or change her or tell her that she should feel anything other than exactly what she is feeling.

It's not my place to tell her man that she should feel any differently than how she feels.

It's not my place to whine, complain or want her to be any different than how she is.

My place is to simply honor her and her partnership with her man.

Every time I arrived to teach Yoga, my car parker friends joked around about how I should hug him.

It's lighthearted, but just to make it crystal clear, one time I said to the man, "I truly respect you, your wife, your agreements and your marriage and I will never hug you, and will never question your wife's wishes because I respect her and all women. You are an incredibly honorable man for honoring her."

Then I told my other friends,

"I honor and respect him, his wife, their agreements and their marriage.

AND, I will give you guys his hugs . . ."

And gave them both an extra hug.

As an honorable woman I want to be trusted.

I want you to feel that I honor you as a woman, your feelings, your partner, your agreements and your relationship.

I want you to feel safe and secure and deeply cared for in my presence.

I want the same for myself.

I will not flirt with your man.

I will not come onto your man.

I will not hug him if you do not want me to.

I won't even talk to him if you do not want me to.

Even if he is one of my dearest friends, if for whatever reason you do not feel comfortable with me being around him, I will honor and respect you and peacefully disengage with him.

That is how deeply I honor and respect a woman's emotions, processes, wishes, intuition and the deep love, devotion and care that she and her man have poured into their relationship.

All women everywhere deserve to be honored for feeling exactly what they feel.

I do.

I honor and I respect you.

EVERY WOMAN IS A WONDER WOMAN

Every woman is a wonder woman.

Every time you love, you're a wonder woman.

Every time you say, "I am so sorry," you're a wonder woman.

Every time you forgive, you're a wonder woman.

Every time you are vulnerable, you're a wonder woman.

Every time you are humble, you're a wonder woman.

Every time you cry, you're a wonder woman.

Every time you laugh, you're a wonder woman.

Every time you roar, you're a wonder woman.

Every time you feel exactly what you feel, you're a wonder woman.

Every time you ask for help, you're a wonder woman.

Every time you help another, you're a wonder woman.

Every time you are openhearted, you're a wonder woman.

Every time you are confident, you're a wonder woman.

Every time you speak the truth, you're a wonder woman.

Every time you stand up in front of a group of people and express your love and appreciation for anyone, even if you only met them once, you're a wonder woman.

Every time you have the guts to sing or dance or make music or create art in front of others, you're a wonder woman.

Every time you are brave enough to keep your heart open and keep loving even though you've been hurt, you're a wonder woman.

Every time you feel broken and discouraged but keep breathing and do everything you can to simply be present with yourself, you're a wonder woman.

Every time you stay true to yourself even though others judge you, you're a wonder woman.

Every time you accept others as they truly are, you're a wonder woman.

Every time you're empowered, you're a wonder woman.

Every time you never give up, you're a wonder woman.

Every time you are brave and bold and courageous, you're a wonder woman.

Every time others say, "It can't be done. It's impossible," and you do it anyway, you're a wonder woman.

Every time you break the mold, color outside the lines and do anything in your 100 percent, one of a kind and unique way, you're a wonder woman.

Every time you face your fear and embrace the great adventure of life, you're a wonder woman.

Every time you tell true life inspirational stories about all the incredible good that is happening in the world and you are one of the characters in the beautiful story, despite the fact that there is so much sadness in the world, you're a wonder woman.

Every time you speak up against injustice and violence in the world, you're a wonder woman.

Every time you stand up for the underdog, you're a wonder woman.

Every time you believe in someone, including yourself, you're a wonder woman.

Every time you love and support another woman, man, child or creature, you're a wonder woman.

Every time you don't dim your light to make others feel more comfortable and less triggered by your beauty, brilliance and God given gifts, you're a wonder woman.

Every time you get triggered or feel uncomfortable in the presence of another's beauty, brilliance and God-given gifts that inspire you to love and support yourself more and shine brighter, you're a wonder woman.

Every time you keep shining in the name of love even though some people think you're a fake or a fraud or conceited or narcissistic because your conscience is crystal clear, you're a wonder woman.

Every time you do and say everything you can to make things right, you're a wonder woman.

Every time you unabashedly speak on behalf of Great Spirit, the Great Mystery and the Benevolent Source, you're a wonder woman.

Every time you channel the Spiritual energy of the Universe, you're a wonder woman.

Every time you remember that you are the daughter of the Benevolent Source and were birthed into this world to make manifest the highest potential of your truest, deepest and highest Self, you're a wonder woman.

Every time you surrender your life to the Benevolent Source so that it can do its work through you, you're a wonder woman.

Every time you make love and open yourself to be truly loved, you're a wonder woman.

Every time you are truly you no matter what, you're a wonder woman.

YOU ARE A WONDER WOMAN.

I AM A WONDER WOMAN.

I LOVE YOU AND I SUPPORT YOU WONDER WOMEN.

THE BEST DAY EVER

Classic interaction at the Church of Trader Joe's:

The super sweet checkout man said,
"Hello there! How are you today?"

I said,
"I am amazing! How are you?"

He said,
"I feel like a bride married to amazement!"

I said,
"Me too! Today is the best day ever!"

He said,
"Remember the conversation between Winnie the Pooh and Piglet?
'What day is it?' asks Pooh.
'It's today!' squeeked Piglet.
'My favorite day!' said Pooh."

I said,

"Yes! I love that story. That's pretty much how I feel every day. And I am always so surprised when people question my happiness, gratitude and pure enthusiasm about life. Every day is a total miracle and there is SO MUCH to be happy about, grateful for and enthusiastic about."

He said,

"Yes! We are so blessed and so lucky!"

I said,

"Yes! We sure are! We are deeply loved, cherished and adored forever. We are so taken care of. The Benevolent Source of the Universe is breathing for us, beating our hearts for us and coursing blood through our veins for us."

He said,

"Do you love Jesus?"

I said,

"Yes! I love Jesus. I love all the Great Masters who have come before us who spoke and acted in alignment with Love, Gratitude, Compassion, Peace and Harmony on behalf of the Benevolent Source."

He said,

"Me too."

I said,

"You are doing a very good job walking in the footsteps of the beautiful path that Jesus walked."

He said,

"Thank you! So are you. So, what is your faith?"

I said,

"I am a Universalist. I believe the core heart and Soul of all religions are the same. When you get back to the essence of all religions, they all recommend the same beautiful ways of living."

He said,

Yes, but do you have one path that you follow?

I said,

"My Spiritual path is truly Universal. I have a BA in Religious Studies and have studied Religion in depth. I once wrote a paper for a class called Religion and Violence. The thesis of the paper was that violence is the secret heart of Religion . . . the most atrocious wars, violence and tragedies in this world have happened because people think that their religion is THE religion and hurt others in the name of God. It's sad but true."

He said,

"Yes, that's true. So what do you believe?"

I said,

"I believe there is a truly loving and caring Benevolent Flow of energy operating through every person, place and thing in existence. I believe that I am here to represent that Benevolent Source in my thoughts, emotions, words and actions, in all of my relationships with all people, places and things, on all levels, planes and dimensions of reality and do my very best to do the work of the Benevolent Source in the world."

He said,

"You're doing a very good job. Thank you!"

I said,

"You're doing a very good job too! Thank you! I love you and I am grateful for you."

He said,

"I love you and I am grateful for you! I really, really love you."

I said,

"Have the best day ever."

He said,

"I am."

Let it be known, no other customers were delayed and the flow of business at Trader Joe's was not upset in any way by we two human beings acting on behalf of the Benevolent Source during the creation of this magical interaction.

Delaying others would have been rude, disharmonious and totally out of alignment with acting on behalf of the Benevolent Force . . . it is important to always be aware of how you are affecting others and their lives.

When a true lady and a true gentleman take the time to connect eye to eye, heart to heart and spirit to spirit, great things can be achieved in the spiritual, emotional, mental and material realms simultaneously.

When you remember that you are a multidimensional physical, mental, emotional and spiritual being you can unload, scan and bag groceries while Soul gazing with your customer, ask deep inquiring questions and be a truly loving gentleman.

When you remember that you are pure light filling up space and that you are made up of the same stuff as the Sun, Moon, Stars, Planets, your groceries and your checkout gentleman, you can swipe your card and give your signature while flowing Universal Love and Universal Truths as all gracious and kind ladies do. When you remember that YOU ARE AN EXTENSION OF PURE BENEVOLENT SOURCE ENERGY and consistently pray every day before you even get out of bed that your thoughts, emotions, words and deeds and that all of your relationships with people, places and things, on all levels, planes and dimensions of reality be led, guided, directed and protected by the Benevolent Source, mountains are moved, seas are parted and time stands still.

As it was clearly demonstrated in this true story, the most important business on this planet is connecting with everyone and everything as an authentic, loving, present, gracious and grateful being.

When we do, all other business that we are engaged in flows with much greater ease, grace, organization, flow and efficiency as it did at Trader Joe's that day.

My entire interaction with him was less than three minutes.

It was not until he was saying the words,

"I really really love you," that another man started to walk up to the checkout stand.

Then I said,

"Have the best day ever."

And he said,

"I am."

At that very moment the new customer handed his groceries to the checkout gentleman and I happily walked away.

Now THAT is the kind of business that we were talking about and that we are both here to do.

And I know with absolute certainty that our interaction improved and up-leveled the quality of everything in my life and his life and the lives of all those who we interact with going forward and the quality of Trader Joe's business.

It's interactions like these that keep me consistently and regularly going back to Trader Joe's. Trader Joe's supplies so many things that I need materially, spiritually, emotionally and mentally and that is why I have given it the well-deserved name THE CHURCH OF TRADER JOE'S.

YOU ARE BEAUTIFUL

One time at the checkout stand at Trader Joe's, I told my lovely checkout lady that she had the most amazing eyelashes and that she was beautiful.

Her entire face lit up. She had a giant smile on her face. She looked like the happiest woman on the planet.

She said,

"Thank you! You made my day! That is so nice of you to say!"

I said,

"AND, you are incredibly sweet and kind and warm too."

She said:

"You are so beautiful and wonderful too and I love your shawl."

I thanked her and we said good-bye and wished each other a wonderful day.

As I turned to walk out of the store, a beautiful woman was also walking toward the exit door.

She looked me right in the eyes and said,

"You are absolutely captivating and I am mesmerized by your colors."

I said,
"Thank you! I am so grateful for your compliment."

She had stunningly beautiful eyes so I said,
"And your beautiful eyes are absolutely mesmerizing."

She said,
"Thank you! That is so sweet."

This entire lovely unfolding of pure feminine, loving, gracious, complimentary and supportive flood of goodness started with one simple sentence:

YOU ARE BEAUTIFUL.

These are the words that females need to hear more than anything. We all need to know that we are lovely, captivating and beautiful, loving, kind and gracious.

Sadly, some people are jealous and envious of beautiful feminine energy and withhold love and compliments or even become competitive and say mean things to the gentle feminine spirit or even worse try to destroy it.

This energy only flows from people who do not feel good about themselves and are threatened by the radiant beauty and grace of the feminine.

It is sad but true.

As we all know, this is not only happening to women and girls, this is happening to our beautiful Mother Earth.

There is something we can do, though, to continuously shift these sad tides and uphold and celebrate the lovely energy of the feminine.

Whenever you are in the presence of beautiful feminine energy, be grateful for it, compliment it and appreciate it.

The feminine lives in us all.

In women, men, children, in all of nature and all of existence.

Love her. Cherish her. Acknowledge her. Tell her every day how stunningly beautiful she is.

This is what she needs more than anything.

Our beautiful world, our lovely Mother Earth is spinning through our galaxy like a lovely girl spinning in a sparkling flowing skirt or a gorgeous woman twirling in a beautiful long dress.

She is doing this to shine her radiant beauty for us.

Tell her how captivatingly beautiful she is and she will keep spinning her beauty for us because she will feel seen, loved, adored and appreciated.

There is a wonderful saying:

LOVE MAKES THE WORLD GO ROUND.

The more we flow love and appreciation to the feminine, the more she shines and glows and flows beauty and grace and sweetness our way and keeps spinning and spinning her captivating magical energy for us all.

It's the best feeling to be in this dance of reciprocal love and appreciation with the feminine.

Thank you in every way and every day that you flow your love and appreciation to the feminine.

REMEMBER TO LOVE AND APPRECIATE YOURSELF TOO.

You are amazing. You are beautiful. I love you and I support you.

YOU ARE AMAZING

There truly is SO MUCH GOODNESS in our beautiful world.

One of my favorite parts of one super sweet and very fun weekend was when I was walking down the street with one of my best friends to frolic at the Summer Solstice gathering at the park and crossed paths with an adorable man who was wearing a full-length rainbow onesie.

I said,

"You are adorable! I love your rainbow onesie!"

He gave me a giant hug, told me he loved me and handed me a sign that said YOU ARE AMAZING to take forth into the world.

From that moment forward I walked around with that sign flashing to every person I saw.

The response was incredible.

Everyone gave me giant smiles.

Lots of people hugged me.

Many people told me they love me.

Everyone said, "YOU ARE AMAZING TOO."

It is SO simple to make a difference.

One smile, one positive message, one hug . . .

That is all it takes to make the day of everyone in your presence.

And you'll make today the best day ever for you too.

YAY!

I love you and I support you.

REPRESENT

One morning at breakfast while I was teaching at the Esalen Institute, I had a super sweet interaction with a man in his seventies who has been coming to Esalen since the '60s.

When he asked me what I was up to this weekend I told him that I was teaching Restorative Yoga, A Journey Through the Chakras, Pranayama Breathwork and Slow Flow Yoga.

He responded by telling me about a few very upsetting experiences that he has had with Yoga in his life and that it left him feeling bad about Yoga.

His stories were a bit intense and he was definitely still a bit triggered and the energy that his story was creating was a bit heavy.

In that moment, despite the somewhat unfavorable things that he was saying about one of my great loves in my life, there was no other place I would have rather been.

I realized that life was giving me an opportunity to turn the love around and provide a different experience of Yoga and Yogis and Yoginis.

My first response was,

"May I give you a hug?"

He said,

"YES!"

When I did, he said,

"I really needed that."

I said,

"We all do."

Then he complained that it seemed that the focus of Yoga was totally on doing physical movement.

I said that in the West the focus of the practice can be very physical but that just because some people approach it as a purely physical practice doesn't mean that we all do.

I said that physical movement is only part of the practice and that the heart of the traditional practice is about uniting the body, mind and heart with the Spirit and our highest potential.

It's a practice of allowing the best, most conscientious and loving part of yourself to guide your thoughts, emotions, words and actions.

He started to soften.

He said that some of the Yogis and Yoginis that he has met were really full of themselves, conceited, cold and acted like they were part of a special club that he was not a part of.

I said that the heart of Yoga is about Unity Consciousness and that we are all in this thing together and that the path of Yoga is inherently about being inclusive with and making peace with all parts of ourselves, with each other and all of existence.

He smiled and it was clear that he was feeling a little bit better about Yoga.

And then the clincher . . .

He said,

"Quite a few times I have been turned away from a class because I can't get off the ground and can't do everything that they do in Yoga. So, I can't do Yoga."

I replied,

"YES, you can. Are you willing to try something with me?"

He replied,

"YES, sure."

I asked him to join me on a bench and did about three minutes of chair Yoga with him.

He said,

"This is Yoga?"

I said,

"It sure is."

He said,

"That feels good. I feel better."

Before he left to attend a workshop about transformation, I apologized on behalf of the tradition and the 5,000 year lineage of Yoga and told him that I was sorry that he had some challenging experiences with Yoga and Yogis and Yoginis and hope that he had more positive experiences of Yoga going forward.

Now and always I am reflecting on how important it is to be a universally positive representative of anything that I do and teach and am feeling more motivated than ever to be a benevolent ambassador of the ancient healing practices that I flow into the world.

Oftentimes, especially when I teach at Esalen, I am teaching to a huge international group of people that I may never see again.

The way that I represent the practices that I am teaching can and will have a lasting impact on them physically, mentally, emotionally and spiritually.

Ultimately, what I flow to those I serve has nothing to do with me at all.

I am simply a grain of sand representing the collective.

It would be a shame if someone was turned off to Yoga or any other powerful lineage because I misrepresented the lineages that I am a part of.

In the big picture, we all represent humanity.

My deep feeling is that we are all in this together.

Every moment and every experience is an opportunity to be a benevolent representative of humanity and all of existence.

More than ever I am devoted to being an inclusive, loving, forgiving, gracious, kind, compassionate, warmhearted, present and grateful human being who makes everyone and everything feel at home and included.

I am here to be of service to the greater good of the collective.
I know you are too.

Thank you for all the love you embody and share.
I love you and I support you.

THE UNIVERSAL LANGUAGE OF THE HEART

I met someone once who had been in an executive position in four different public school districts in and around Santa Barbara, California. When she met me she said that I was very familiar to her.

I smiled and said,

"We have probably seen each other many times in passing at Trader Joe's or the Farmer's Market."

Then I asked her,

"Have you practiced much Yoga? I have been a Yoga teacher for a long time and that's how a lot of people know me."

She said no.

She asked me,

"Have you ever been a public school teacher in Santa Barbara?"

I said,

"Well, I started the first ever Yoga in the schools program in Santa Barbara in 2000."

And she said,

"How did that go? Did you ever have trouble with the parents? We have had repeated problems with parents complaining that they think that Yoga is a Religion and we had to stop a lot of the classes."

I said,

"In the twelve years that I taught up to fifteen classes a week in the Public and Private schools of Santa Barbara and the eighteen trainings that I did teaching Yoga teachers and school teachers how to teach Yoga to kids, I never had one complaint about the classes.

The only comment I ever heard was from a parent who said,

"My son keeps singing a song that you taught him that goes

'The light in me sees the light in you.'

Is that some kind of spiritual thing?

Because if it is I don't feel comfortable with my boy singing that song."

I replied,

"Science has proven that we are all made of atoms and atoms are continuously giving off, and absorbing, light and energy, all the time, so, at an atomic level, seeing the light in each other is a universal truth. And it also means that all of the good stuff in me sees all the good stuff in you."

She replied,

"Okay. That makes sense and I understand now and feel comfortable with him singing the song."

More than ever I am so grateful that I trained myself to transform the way I language things when I go into mainstream settings so that I can bring much needed esoteric wisdom, health and wellness practices into mainstream settings like the schools and the Cancer Center.

When I taught people how to teach Yoga to kids this was a big part of my training.

The way we say things can create connection or separation and because of the separation of Church and State it is important for teachers who teach Yoga in the schools to honor this law and therefore honor all people of all religions.

It's sad to think that something as wonderful as Yoga could be shut down in a school because parents think it's a religion.

More than ever we all need tools to help us navigate through these challenging times more healthfully, mindfully and peacefully. Mainstream settings such as schools, hospitals, financial institutions, political arenas, etc., need Self-Care practices too.

I am more motivated than ever when I am in mainstream settings to speak a nondogmatic Universal language of connection and kindness that is universally understood and received and that everyone who hears it receives the feeling of warmth, care and compassion through the words I speak and the practices I teach.

EVERYONE HAS A HEART and when we speak the universal language of the Heart we can help to activate it in every heart that we meet and in any setting.

EVERY DAY IS A PEACE MARCH

One time on my way up the mountain to my home after going to the Farmer's Market, I came upon a giant delivery truck whose back end was stuck on the upward slanting hill.

I stopped to give my condolences to the delivery man by saying,

"Oh man . . . that sucks. I'm sorry about that."

The delivery man said,

"Awww, Miss. Thank you. We have been stuck here for four hours waiting for a tow truck to come help us out. Now our entire day is running late and our deliveries to everyone are going to be late."

I said,

"Okay, my friend, I am going to vision that the tow truck gets here ASAP so that you can get on with your day and your deliveries."

He said,

"Thank you, sweetheart. I am hoping for the same thing."

We said our good-byes and I was on my way.

Forty-five minutes later after dropping my produce off in my fridge and doing some things around the house, I headed back down the hill to go to a Peace March and came upon the stuck delivery truck and the delivery man again.

The tow truck had just arrived and he was getting the help he had been waiting for.

I slowed down to tell him how happy I was for him and before I could say a word, he walked up to my car and said,

"Miss, I only met you for a minute, but this I know for sure: We need more people like you in the world. You really helped me feel better and now look! Right after we spoke the tow truck arrived and pretty soon we are going to get on with our day. Thank you. You are such a sweetheart."

I said,

"And you are such a kind and gracious gentleman. We need more bighearted men like you in the world. I am grateful for you and I am happy that you are such an exemplary role model for mankind. Thank you."

On the mountain and down in the town . . .

Women, men and children can march together for peace, love and kindness anytime and everywhere.

EVERY DAY AND EVERYWHERE IS THE PEACE MARCH.

LOVE FIRST

A friend once asked me if I have held back with the advancement of my career because of my relationship with my man.

And I said,

"YES. For sure."

For me, building anything, especially a career, is not worth it unless the foundation of it is LOVE.

Love for my man. Love for my family. Love for my friends. And of course Self-Love and Self-Care.

One of the core reasons that I created my Life Coaching and Lifestyle Program is because I have met so many visionaries, leaders and teachers with rockin' careers and missions who are doing great work in the world, but at a fundamental level are not truly happy because they have neglected their intimate relationships with their partners, friends and family and have neglected their relationship with themselves.

I call it putting the cart before the horse.

And what ends up happening is that when we live this way we eventually burn out and our Souls buck because at some fundamental level we know that we are missing the mark.

I know how this feels because this is exactly how I felt in my life many years ago.

My body was suffering. I was extremely overweight. I was in an unhealthy relationship. My long-term friendships were waning. I was struggling with my family. And, I felt like a fraud. Because I was not living in alignment with everything that I taught and truly believe in.

So I decided to make some radical changes so that I would have a sense of true balance in my life.

And this is the magical thing . . .

The more that I prioritize Love and time for my man, family, friends and my foundational self-love and care, the deeper and more sustainable my roots are and the more fulfilling and prosperous my career is and the happier I am.

I am into slow growth now.

I am devoted to sustainability every day.

I want the real deal.

And I am willing to wait and be patient and practice taking care of what truly matters on a daily basis so that anything that I grow is flowing from the deep place of Love within me.

And even though I don't have to choose, if I had to, I would choose home and hearth and love and partnership and friends and family any day over being the rock star of the world in my career.

A career where in any way I have to sacrifice a foundation of deep love and connection with my loved ones is definitely not worth it. That's way too big a price to pay.

So today, I feel really blessed because I am really clear about what matters most.

And the super sweet thing is the more I take care of what matters most and give ample time to cultivate love with my man, friends and family,

the more

I am healthy. I am happy. And I continuously attract amazing people to work with that share the same values and my career continues to blossom beautifully.

I love you and support you and am visioning all your dreams coming true too.

THE ELEVATOR ANGEL

I was waiting for an elevator one day and a tall dapper man, who I am pretty sure was in his seventies and who I had never met before, approached the elevators and started to walk very slowly in a very dramatic, theatrical and playful way.

When he reached me and the elevators he said,

"I had to really slow down as I was approaching the elevator zone because these elevators are really slow."

Then he said,

"How are you?"

And took my hand and looked me in the eyes and said,

"Are you good? Are you married?"

I knew he wasn't hitting on me although he had a very flirtatious nature.

He was sincerely connecting with me.

And I instantly knew that he felt that the indicator of being good is when you are in a deeply committed relationship with someone you love.

I smiled and said,

"I am not married, but I have an amazing boyfriend and we have a very loving partnership and I feel like a very lucky lady to be with him."

He squeezed my hand, winked, smiled and said,
"Good. He is a very lucky man."

I said,
"And you? Are you married?"

He said,
"Yes, for fifty-five years. And we have six children and six grandchildren."

And I said,
"Then you're not only good. You're REALLY good."

And he said,
"Yes, I am a very lucky man."

I said,
"Yes, and she is a very lucky lady. And so are those six children and six grandchildren."

Then his elevator that was going up arrived. And my elevator that was going down arrived.

I looked at him and said,
"Stay kind and loving. You're a very good man."

And then he gave me that smile and wink again and said, "You're a very good lady. Stay pretty."

That made me giggle.

As I reflect on this beautiful, sweet and fun interaction that I had with this vivacious elder, it feels like I was given such a pure and innocent message:

Having good and loving harmonious relationships is the indication of a good and happy life.

Simple human Love is truly the most important part of our lives. I am grateful that I have a loving partner, family, friends, students and clients and that we share our love with each other.

And I am super grateful for my elevator Angel who reminded me of the pure innocent goodness of strangers who graciously share their love and wisdom with me every single day.

THE MOST COURTEOUS AWARD

Have you noticed that things are a bit wild out in the world right now?

Even cruising around a small town like Santa Barbara, I could feel the energy ramping up as we approached Thanksgiving and the Holidays one year.

There was a lot of rushing, honking and some frustrated people out there.

My feeling is that a lot of people start to feel a tremendous amount of internal and external pressure when the Holiday season arrives.

And it took some extra compassion out there in the collective that day to stay centered and at ease.

At one point I was turning off a very busy road into a very busy shopping center and ended up behind a very disgruntled man driving a convertible.

He was shaking his head from side to side and threw his arms up in the air in a very dramatic way.

I could palpably feel his upset energy.

In that moment I clearly felt two parts of myself:

There was part of me that thought:

Take it easy Mr.!

And that part of me was being slightly judgmental . . . Well, maybe more than slightly.

And there was another part of me that thought:

I have no idea what happened to him today or what he is going through and we all have days that are super challenging.

In that moment I had a choice.

Choose judgment . . .

Or choose compassion.

By now, I have trained for these daily moments and I know what judgment does to me. It makes me feel awful. I have chosen to practice compassion over and over and it makes me feel really good.

And I was having a good day and didn't want to allow someone else's energy to lower my vibration. I wanted to maintain my good vibes.

So, I took a deep breath in and a slow breath out and practiced what I practice in meditation every day and silently sent him this message:

I love you. I am sorry that life is frustrating you today. Please forgive me for anything I am doing in the world that in any way is adding to your collective troubles. I am grateful for you and am sending you positive energy and support to get through the rest of your day more peacefully.

Within moments he put on his blinker and was waiting for a parking space so I very slowly drove around him and started singing my Parking Angel song to manifest a parking spot . . . anyone who has ever been in the car with me in a parking lot has heard this song and usually sings along . . . because it's really cute.

The Parking Angel was on it and within moments someone pulled out of their parking space about ten feet in front of me and thirty feet in front of him.

As soon as I saw that parking spot open up, I thought that giving him the parking spot would be going beyond sending him positive energy and would be the best way to SHOW HIM that I care about him.

I stopped my car, leaned out the window and said,

"Would you like this parking spot?"

He nodded YES.

I drove on knowing that another spot would be there for me and he took the one I offered.

I immediately found another parking spot and as I was walking through the parking lot, he stopped me by saying,

"Are you the lady who just gave me that parking spot?"

I said, "YES."

He said,

"Well, in a world of many people who don't seem to care, you do, and I am giving you the MOST COURTEOUS AWARD" and gave me a big smile.

In return, I gave him a big hug and said,

"Thank you. I love you. At the end of the day and at the end of this life, moments of Love and Kindness are what we will truly remember. Everything else fades away. Being loving and kind is how we can all truly make a difference. Thank you for being so loving, kind and courteous too."

He said, "Thank you. You turned my day around. Happy Thanksgiving. I am grateful for you."

What I did and said clearly helped him feel better and maybe restored some of his faith in humanity, which was really sweet . . . but that is not the only thing that felt good.

The thing that felt really good was consciously choosing kindness when I easily could have chosen to be judgmental.

Being stubborn, self-righteous and greedy was right there ready to be chosen.

But I made a choice that I have come to know over time makes me feel good about myself, humanity and life.

We all have these choice points all the time in any given day.

But we have to be in the right frame of body/mind/heart/ spirit in order to consciously choose the way of being that is most beneficial for ourselves and all of existence.

Most days I eat really clean organic homemade food.

I get great nights of deep sleep.

Most mornings I wake up, talk to my boyfriend, tidy up the house, have a cup of tea, write in my journal and schedule my entire day.

I take a sauna where I sweat out toxins and impurities, relax, do breath work, meditate, do emotional cleansing practices and pray to be guided by my highest, truest and deepest self every day.

I do some yoga and other forms of exercise.

Most days I talk to or spend time with friends and talk about everything (the good and the challenging) that is happening in our lives.

We connect, bond, love and support each other.

Then I serve the people that need me.

I take good care of myself.

When that moment arrived when I encountered that man in the parking lot, I had already conditioned myself to respond the way I responded.

I remember countless times in similar situations where I was not regularly eating healthfully, exercising, meditating, breathing, clearing heavy emotions, resting, relaxing and getting enough sleep.

During those times my reaction to that day's encounter was sometimes different.

I might have put on a happy face but inside I was sometimes pissed, frustrated and judgmental.

And I did not like how I felt.

So I started to change all the little things that I knew might make me feel happier and more peaceful.

Now, when I shift the way I eat, move, breathe, rest, etc., it always has a HUGE IMPACT on not only how I feel physically, mentally, emotionally and spiritually inside but it also greatly impacts the way that I show up in the world.

When people ask me what the benefits of my work are and want to know about some of the positive changes that people have experienced, I share stories like this.

Everything I experienced in that parking lot is the direct result of what I practice every day and continual practice is what it takes to be a conscientious person.

Your daily practice helps you be an Angel to everyone everywhere you go too.

THE PEACE RALLY

I was walking through the Trader Joe's parking lot with flowers in my hands.

After putting the flowers in the car, a woman with black hair and olive skin who was sitting in the passenger seat next to her husband in their car called me over.

In a very thick and definitely not American accent, she said, "Why do you have those flowers?"

I said,
"I have them because I love them and they are beautiful."

English was very clearly not her primary language and she misunderstood me in the sweetest way possible.

She responded,
"You think I am beautiful?"

And without missing a beat I said,
"Yes, I do. You are very beautiful."

She said,

"Thank you, but I still don't understand why people have flowers. I just saw a lady with so many flowers in her grocery cart. Why do you think she had all those flowers?"

I said,

"Well, maybe she likes flowers a lot too. Maybe she is having a big party and wants to decorate her home with them so that it looks super beautiful. Maybe they are a gift for someone."

And she said,

"A gift? You think she might give all those flowers away?"

I said,

"Maybe so.

One day I was at the Farmer's Market and a man walked up to me with a giant bunch of flowers. I did not know him and he gave me a flower. He was giving flowers to everyone at the Farmer's Market. I thanked him, gave him a hug and told him I loved him and he told me that he loved me."

She said,

"You gave a man you didn't know a hug and told him that you loved him?"

And I said,

"Yes, I did. And even though I have never met you before, I love you too."

With tears in her eyes she gently touched her heart and said,

"You have touched my Heart. You are speaking to me the way God speaks to me. I feel his love coming through you."

I said,

"God bless you. God and I love you."

And she said,

"I love you too."

Shortly thereafter a friend texted me from a huge Peace
Rally in downtown Santa Barbara.

My new friend and I were at a Peace Rally too. . . .
You don't have to go to a Peace Rally to rally for peace.
It can happen anywhere.

Today, two strangers of two different colors from two
different countries chose Love and rallied for Peace right in
the middle of the TJ's parking lot.

KEEP THE FIRE BURNING

Almost every day I make a fire or at least I light a candle every day.

One day I made a fire and I worked fireside for most of the day. It was warm and magical.

At one point the fire had totally gone out and all that was left were some burning coals.

At first I thought I was going to have to completely overhaul my entire fire to make the flames come back.

But all I did was move one log ever so slightly and, like magic, the entire fire started blazing fully again.

It has served as a powerful metaphor for anything and everything in life.

Sometimes we think that we have lost the flame in any given area of our lives and worry that we are going to have to do a massive overhaul to bring back the energy and vitality to that part of our lives.

But oftentimes simply one small change, like a shift in perception or approaching life in a new and different way, is required.

I am visioning the fires that you are cultivating in your life blazing brightly and that you remember that small changes make big changes.

YOUR HIGHER SELF IS CALLING

There comes a day when you get clear, make a choice and decide: I don't want to live this way anymore.

I want THIS now.

You stop flowing your energy toward thoughts, emotions, words, actions, people, places and things that are not aligned with what you know in the core of your innermost being is aligned with your greatest health, happiness and harmony.

You start flowing all of your energy toward cultivating thoughts, emotions, words, actions and relationships with people, places and things that are aligned with what you know in the core of your innermost being support, enhance and uplift your highest and best good and therefore the highest and best good of all of existence.

When you get clear and make this choice,

Your life will become a unique, one of a kind and beautiful work of art that only you can create by being you.

You will perpetually move in the direction of being a Master of yourself, your thinking, your emotions, your words and your actions.

You will begin to feel and know with your whole heart that you are creating a Masterpiece out of your life because you are being the best you that you can possibly be every single day.

You will create a Masterpiece by being a Master of Peace.

You will be a Master of Peace because you feel in every cell of your body that you have done the very best that you can possibly do today and this inner knowing will activate the true embodiment of pure peace.

And you are the only one who knows these deep internal truths.

There is no other who knows what True Self Mastery is for you other than you.

You cannot fool yourself.

When you make the choice to always move in the direction of living in alignment with True Self Mastery,

Things are going to be different.

Because you will no longer be indifferent.

You will be different because you will care deeply about being the best you that you can possibly be every single day.

And then you can truly make a difference in the world.

Being the best you that you can possibly be is the single greatest gift that you can possibly give the world.

When you make this choice,

You will be living in a whole new world.

And you will help to birth the new world of true universal health, prosperity, creativity, cooperation, power, love, happiness, harmony, authenticity, peace and enlightenment, one and for all.

Today is the day when you can draw the line and align with your highest potential.

In so doing, you will help all beings everywhere do the same.

You are that powerful.

Your Higher Self is calling you today . . .

And it's a wake-up call.

Let's do this.

EVERYONE IS A LEADER

One day I was at the Church of Trader Joe's where
I consistently have beautiful high vibe spiritual experiences . . .
like getting carded and meeting Earth Angels.

My super sweet checkout guy was asking me what I was
up to today and, when I told him I was going to watch the
Presidential Debate, the next lady in line picked up her
bottle of two-buck Chuck wine and said,

"That's why I am getting this! And I am going to be drinking
it alone because none of my friends will get near me right
now because I am so vocal about the election."

And then she started going off a lil bit.

And the checkout guy said,

"It's a total fiasco and I can't believe it's happening . . . I saw
a list of quotes of all the Presidents in US history and, when you
get the quotes of one of the current Presidential candidates,
it's unbelievable that this person is even running for President.

And I said,

"Two of my very favorite quotes by a Leader was Gandhi
who said, 'If the people lead, the leaders will follow and Be
the change you want to see in the world . . .'

So no matter what has come before us and no matter what is happening today, I am going to be a Leader of Love and be the change I want to see in the world."

And the lady said,

"I want to go home with her!"

And the checkout guy said,

"Yes! That's it!"

And I said,

"I love you and I support you in being the powerful Leaders that you are. Together we can do this."

And they both said,

"Yes we can. Thank you."

We don't have to be a President, a King, a Queen, a millionaire or famous to make a positive change and be a Leader.

We don't have to be victims either.

It's our choice.

We can be Leaders right now.

Even in the checkout line at the Church of Trader Joe's.

FLOWER POWER

I was walking into the Farmer's Market one day and I had a premonition that a man I didn't know was going to walk up to me and give me the gift of a flower.

Within two minutes a young, smiley man whom I have never met before walked up to me and handed me a perfectly lovely hot pink Gerbera daisy.

I thanked him and asked him if I could give him a hug.

He said,

"YES please!"

As I hugged him heart-to-heart I said,

"I love and appreciate you and all the positive energy you are sharing today."

And he said,

"Awwww! I love you too and am grateful for all the positive energy that you are sharing today. I have given away one hundred flowers today and out of one hundred people you are one of three people that gave me a hug and the only one that told me you love me."

I said,

"Well, let's keep spreading the love, flowers and good vibes brother!"

Within a few minutes as I was standing with some friends who have two lovely little girls, he walked up and gave them flowers and in addition added the new gift of telling all of us that he loved us and we told him that we loved him."

He started the positive vibe and we added to it and from there it is continuing to grow, evolve and expand forever.

As you know, I am always sharing super positive everyday magic stories from my life.

I live these beautiful stories every day and love writing about them and sharing them as one of the countless ways that I can do my part to bring love, light and bliss into the world.

I am in eternal gratitude for all the goodness that flows my way and am happy to be of service to the collective by expanding the magic every day in every way that I can.

During these times when we are all being bombarded with extreme negativity from many people, places and things in the collective we have powerful opportunities every day and in every way to bring balance, harmony and goodness to the collective.

I thank each and every one of you who is embodying the energy of Love, Compassion, Truth, Integrity, Universal Goodness and Peace for all of existence here on the planet and in your everyday life.

More than ever your uplifting and positive stories are needed here and I love you and support you every time you share the good vibes with us all.

Thank you.

WABI SABI

You just never know how your day is going to unfold . . .

For many moons I had deeply wanted to visit the Gamble House in Pasadena, a Greene and Greene designed craftsman house and at last I made plans to visit there with my Mama Bird.

We had planned the trip many months in advance and were so looking forward to our adventure together.

The Gamble House's interior exceeded my expectations and I was in awe of the incredible design that was specifically made to bring the feeling of nature indoors.

About twenty minutes into the tour a lady left one of the rooms that we were visiting and her husband followed her out.

I instantly felt like something was amiss with her.

When I walked out into the hallway, I tuned into her energy and felt that something was really out of balance with her and then heard her say to her husband,

"I feel dizzy."

I asked her if she was okay and she said,

"Yes, just a little dizzy."

It was 105 degrees in Pasadena and the skies had been smoky and ashy due to a huge fire in Santa Clarita.

I thought she might be dehydrated or overheated.

All I knew was something was really off.

My intuition told me to go up to her again and encourage her to sit down and rest and hold her hand and give her water and breathe with her but I questioned myself because that might feel invasive to her and I wanted to give her space.

We visited another room and then another and then we all heard a giant crash in the hallway.

I instantly knew what had happened.

I bolted out of the room and into the hallway and she was lying facedown, passed out.

I ran to her and started talking normally to her as if she were conscious, present and awake.

She was nearly gagging and barely breathing and her husband had no idea what to do.

He was in a bit of shock.

No one had any idea what to do.

But I did.

I rushed to her and told her,

"We are here. You are safe. All is well. We are going to slowly turn you over. Ready?"

And then we gently turned her over and I held her head in my hands and gave her Cranial Sacral healing.

I said,

"Breathe. Listen to your breath. Feel the Earth beneath you holding you and supporting you. All is well."

And she did.

She opened her eyes and said,

"What happened?"

We said,

"You passed out."

She said,

"I did?"

I said,

"Yes. But all is well. You are fine. Your husband is here. Keep breathing."

And I asked him to place his hands on her heart . . . and he did.

She said,

"I am sorry."

I said,

"There is nothing to be sorry about. We are here for you."

And she was coming back online.

She said to her husband,

"I'm sorry."

She said,

"We have wanted to come here for a very long time . . . and it's our twenty-eighth wedding anniversary . . . I am sorry that this is happening. I don't know what happened."

I said,

"Ahhhhh . . . Happy Anniversary. Thank you for being longtime lovers. We are grateful for all the love you are bringing to our world."

They both thanked me.

I said,

"Oh, so now I understand why you passed out. After twenty-eight years of marriage you are still so in love that you went weak in the knees and passed out."

They both smiled big smiles.

The entire left side of her face was swelling.

She pulled a chip of tooth out of her mouth and she said her jaw hurt.

I put my hands on her jaw and sent her healing light.

An out of breath woman showed up from somewhere and said,

"I am a nurse."

We welcomed her and thanked her for coming.

She started asking questions.

The nurse asked,

"What is your name?"

She answered.

The nurse asked,
"Who is the president of the United States?"

She paused and then said,
"Well, hopefully the next President of the United States is going to be Hillary Clinton and NOT Donald Trump."

We all giggled and I said,
"You are really going to be just fine."

My Mama Bird popped her head out of the tour several times to look in on us. I knew she had my back 100 percent. I knew she knew what I was doing. Afterward she told me that she knew I would be there and I would help in any way that I could because that is who I am.

And we need that. When we are expanding to be of service, we need Beloveds who totally get us and support us and hold an anchor for us. My Mom was that anchor for me that day and I am grateful to have a Mom who gets it. I am blessed.

I reassured her,
"I've passed out before."

I told her,
"One time when I was in Delhi I ate some bad Matar Paneer, a cheese and pea dish.

The next day while exchanging money at American Express on a super hot day like today I passed out and woke up to thirty tourists surrounding me.

Apparently I lost control of the entire lower half of my body because when I stood up and walked out I left a trail of peas behind me.

Some leave a trail of peace behind them. That day I left a trail of peas."

We all giggled.

Then the paramedics came to check out her vitals and then helped her down the stairs.

Her husband thanked me and I wished them Happy Anniversary again and told him that they would be in my heart and prayers.

When I returned to the tour, our tour guide was talking about the Japanese concept of Wabi Sabi, one of my long-time favorite parts of Japanese art.

Wabi Sabi is something that all Japanese artists weave into everything that they do.

Wabi Sabi means that nothing in life, nature or art is perfect.

Wabi Sabi is the art of representing chaos in nature and life.

Wabi Sabi is purposefully messing something up in your art piece so that it's not perfect because nothing is perfect.

We have plans and life just simply is and it is not always what we planned.

And that's a good thing.

And . . .

We do need a Vision. We do need goals. We do need a plan.

If we didn't make reservations months in advance to go to the Gamble House, then I would not have been there and she might have been laying there facedown barely breathing for too long with no one knowing what to do or how to help her.

And, if I had cared more about sticking to the plan of being on the tour than helping her, then she might not have received the care that she needed.

So we need to be flexible. We need to course correct.

We need to make ourselves available when people need help and give what we can give and help however we can help.

Today was a full circle day for me.

When I was in Peru once, after doing the same for people that were suffering, I was told I had too much empathy and that empathy was my weak link.

When a new friend was hitting a mega rough spot and was sobbing in fetal position on the Earth, I went to her, lay down behind her, spooned and held her tight while she cried and cried and cried until she came through the darkness into the Light.

On that same day another new friend wanted to leave our group because she did not feel included and I felt her Spirit floating away from us.

I prayed for her and sent her love and light. I gave her a gift. I told her she was in my heart. I told her that she matters. I told her I love her and I support her and I see who she is. And she stayed.

I had just met these sweet ones but they and their feelings mattered to me.

I give what I can give, my gift, my love, my compassion, my empathy, my comfort, my support . . . because I gave them the heart of my heart's heart, I was told that I had too much empathy.

When my clients and students cry, I sometimes cry too because more often than not I can relate to how they feel and keeping a stiff upper lip and holding back tears for the sake of "professionalism" for me is not truly helpful and it's not truly human.

I have empathy because I have suffered. I have empathy because I can relate to how they feel.

While in Peru for that one day I humbly opened up to the perspective that perhaps I have too much empathy. . . .

But you know what I discovered?

Lack of empathy and compassion is why all the shit that is going down in the world is going down.

And I have a lot of empathy for the one that told me I have too much empathy.

Clearly that one has not felt the level of pain that many have felt so empathy might not feel possible to that person at this point in their life.

Once you have felt that kind of pain YOU HAVE TO HELP THOSE THAT ARE SUFFERING and you say and do whatever it takes to help relieve them of their suffering.

Life is random and wild and free and chaotic and crazy sometimes. Life is Wabi Sabi.

But if we all greet life with the Spirit of presence, love, compassion, empathy and service with the willingness to serve the hierarchy of needs of everyone and serve the collective, then together we can get through it all with more ease and more grace.

And our conscience, hearts, minds and bodies will be clear, luminous and full of immeasurable LOVE so that even greater LOVE, compassion and goodness can flow through us.

This is the Truth.

This is my Vision.

This is my prayer.

LOVE is our Medicine.

Compassion is our superpower.

Empathy is one of the greatest gifts you can give someone.

Today is your work of art.

Make it beautiful . . . imperfections and all.

Please.

Keep giving everything that you have to give.

We all need each other's gifts more than ever.

KALI-FORNIA

More and more it is dawning on me that apparently we Californians have a rather different worldview than a lot of our fellow American Brothers and Sisters.

The majority of Californians wanted to legalize Marijuana, ban plastic bags and wanted the first woman ever to be our President.

So I now refer to our beautiful state as KALI-fornia.

KALI is the Great Fierce Mother Goddess who is devoted to protecting and taking good care of her children regardless of their political orientation, gender, sexual orientation, spirituality and religion.

KALI loves all of her children equally.

AND she does not appreciate any of her children fighting and judging each other and gets really pissed when they do. She is the one who amidst that darkness comes in and says,

"WAKE UP KIDS!"

It's time to open our hearts and make choices that are aligned with unity so that we can all get along.

She's like a bad-ass protective Mama Bear who keeps us all aligned with the best version of ourselves and gives us a lil pat on the booty when we are acting out of alignment with the universal highest and best good for all.

Some people say that the times we are all living in right now is called KALI-Yuga, or the time of great darkness. It's also revered as being the time when we can catapult ourselves and make leaps and bounds in our spiritual evolution.

Amongst the darkness of hatred, violence, apathy and indifference, this is the time when choosing Love, Compassion, Truth, Justice, Equality, Presence, Peace and Kindness can make all the difference in our own lives and in the collective consciousness.

AND WHEN WE CHOOSE LOVE,

It's darkness before the dawn time.

It's out of the darkness comes the light time.

It's out of the turd comes the Lotus time.

It's pressure makes diamonds time.

CLEARLY, it's KALI-Yuga.

Clearly we have an amazing opportunity to grow and evolve as Human beings and Spiritual beings at lightning speed right now. So, my dear KALI-fornia friends and all American and Global Brothers and Sisters across the world who are devoted to peace amongst the peoples, let's do our best to BE KIND to everyONE.

Smile.

Wave.

Say hello.

Give a hug.

Ask, "How are you?"

Say, "Thank you."

Give a buck.

Give a fuck.

Don't be indifferent. Be different. Make a difference.

Everyone needs those of us who can BE KIND to BE KIND.

Thank you Brave Hearts.

I love you and I support you through the darkness into the Light.

INTEGRATION

Twelve days after returning from one of my trips to Peru, I was still deeply INTEGRATING everything that I went through on my epic adventure.

One of the ways that I INTEGRATE is by taking time to be in nature and the mountains.

In Peru the mountains are called Apus and are considered great and powerful guardians and guides who can help you stand tall in the presence of your purpose, values and big Vision for your life like a mighty mountain.

The Mountain Apu spirits of Santa Barbara that are sometimes cloaked in mystical clouds in the morning help me to stay connected with my own higher purpose, values and Vision for my life and help me to embody and ground all the teachings I received in Peru.

INTEGRATION is one of the core practices that I practice and that I recommend my students and clients practice and that I incorporate into all of my classes, workshops, trainings and retreats because it is so vitally important.

When we go through peak experiences such as a yoga class, hiking up a mountain, a coaching session, a deep conversation, making love, running a marathon, visiting a sacred site, celebrating a birthday or holiday, experiencing a spiritual ceremony or any of the other peak experiences that we may experience in a given day/week/ month/year/lifetime, we need time to process it all.

We need to take time to notice what we have learned, be aware of what we'd like to shift next time we experience a similar peak experience, take notes or journal, sleep, discuss it with our teacher, coach, friend or in a sharing circle so that our experience doesn't become just another peak and then falls and fade away.

The true gift of a peak experience is when you go through a physical, mental, emotional or spiritual transformation and then maintain the turning point you experienced by fully embodying those profound changes in your day-to-day life.

We live in a world where we are oftentimes encouraged to keep pushing and keep gathering and keep manifesting and keep making it happen but we are rarely encouraged to stop, reflect, feel, process, talk about it, relax and replenish.

The go go go without the pause for digestion and integration is a recipe for fatigue, burn out and eventual exhaustion and we end up losing the very gifts that we received during the peak experiences. I have experienced this myself in the past and I have witnessed it in countless friends, family, students and clients.

I love that the word INTEGRITY and INTEGRATION are so similar.

In my opinion and in my experience, Leaders, Teachers, Visionaries and Healers who give themselves and their students and clients the necessary gift of INTEGRATION are modeling right energy and upholding INTEGRITY in the collective consciousness.

I am visioning you taking the time to INTEGRATE all of the amazing experiences that you have today and every day.

EYES OF LOVE

After teaching Pranayama and Slow Flow Yoga one morning at the Esalen Institute, I met two lovely men from Persia in the hot springs.

They were Lovers and artists and healers and it was clear that they were in Love.

And they were very beautiful Souls, inside and out.

In their presence I felt like I was in the presence of Rumi and his Beloved Friend . . . and I couldn't tell who was Rumi and who was the Beloved friend because it felt like they had merged and become One.

This felt like a sublime blessing and a special gift because I am a lifetime Lover of Love, loving and Rumi, one of the greatest Lovers and Lovers of Love that has ever loved.

When you are in the presence of two people who have surrendered fully to Love, as these two Lovers have, they as individuals seem to dissolve into Love and have become Love itself . . . and one cannot tell anymore who is the Lover and who is the Beloved.

And who cares? Because the Love that flows through them is all that can be felt. And the Love that is, is all that truly matters.

When one of them first spoke to me it was as if Rumi himself was writing a Love poem just for me and it evoked the same lyrical sweetness out of me so that when I spoke I felt like my words were an offering placed on their Altar of Love in the Temple of the Lovers.

When one of them first spoke, he looked with his golden brown eyes into my golden brown eyes, and tenderly said,

"I feel like I know you. I feel like we have met before. I feel like we have always known each other. I feel like you have always been here."

And his Love looked with his golden brown eyes into my golden brown eyes, and tenderly said,

"Yes, this is how I feel too."

And I felt seen and loved, like they knew who I am and they knew why I am here.

And I looked with my golden brown eyes into their golden brown eyes, and tenderly said,

"Yes, this is how I feel too. And I feel like we all feel this way about each other because we are looking at each other with the eyes of Love."

And they both said,

"Yes, that is it . . . we all see each other with eyes of Love."

And we all smiled with soft and knowing smiles of Love.

There is a way of looking at each and every person, place and thing in existence with the gentle eyes of Universal Love.

Seeing the best in every person, place and thing.

Seeing the Heart in every person, place and thing.

Seeing the goodness in every person, place and thing.

Seeing the Love in every person, place and thing.

More than ever, my prayer, my Vision and my wish is that each and every one of us awakens from the dream of separation and continuously opens our Heart and opens our eyes and gazes in awe, wonder and Love at each other and recognizes that the most beautiful person, place and thing is standing before us in each and every moment.

AIN'T NOTHIN GONNA BREAK MY STRIDE

After experiencing disappointments when things don't manifest in the way that I planned, expected and wanted, I do my best to use the experience as an opportunity to up-level the way that I live my own life.

Abraham-Hicks says that life is like a giant buffet of incredibly diverse people/places/things/experiences.

When we experience something from the buffet of life that doesn't "taste" good energetically to us it's an opportunity to get even more clear about what does taste good to us energetically.

Nothing is inherently right or wrong . . . we all just have different energetic tastebuds.

When we experience contrast to what tastes good to us energetically, rockets of desire are set off to create the exact opposite of what we are experiencing: a delicious tasting life that resonates with our truest, deepest and highest purpose, values and big Vision.

So after having experiences when I have felt like people that I trust are not keeping their word, not respecting my time, energy and resources, not being responsible for creating sacred space before and after peak physical/emotional/ mental/spiritual experiences through proper preparation and integration time, cheating, seducing, being irreverent, being manipulative, etc., I experience a lot of contrast to what I uniquely value and vision for myself personally.

As one of my teachers once said,

"Don't just trust people. Know people."

In other words, Don't live life in blind Faith. Pay attention to what people actually do and how they actually behave. Know them for how they actually show up, not how you would like them to show up.

Of course, I have 0 percent control over anyone and their actions. If I try to change others, then it's a never ending cycle of suffering.

And, if I do nothing and take no action, then I end up feeling frustrated too.

So I use contrast as an opportunity to change myself because I do have 100 percent control over my own actions.

The Truth is, if one thing on the buffet table is not tasty, then it's my responsibility to spit it out and be open to eating something that is actually nourishing and yummy for me.

It's not the yucky tasting tidbits responsibility to change the way it tastes . . . it's just simply being and tasting like what it is.

Changing myself had been my practice over the past few days after I arrived home after two and a half weeks in Peru where I experienced an entire buffet of experiences, some of which were the most delicious tastes I have ever tasted and some that I tried to digest despite the fact that I didn't like the way they tasted at all and they literally made me sick.

During my second trip to Peru, I designed a pair of pants (did you know I am a fashion designer and also used to walk down a lot of runways?) but didn't start to make them until the day before I left for Peru and didn't finish them before I left.

I had not kept my word to myself to make the pants. I had not respected the muse that gave me the idea. I had not respected my time, energy and resources. I had not maintained the turning point by integrating the idea that came to me during my peak experience of inspiration and creativity by actually making them.

So when I arrived home from Peru I got out my sewing machine and finished them.

They are blue jean bell-bottom pants with vintage Peruvian blanket panels that go down the sides of the legs and I love them.

They are metaphorical pants for me.

You know that saying,

Put on your big girl panties and deal with it?

Well, these are my "Deal with it" pants.

They represent me dealing with all of the people/places/things that disappoint and frustrate me.

Instead of staying stuck in the "That's wrong" story, I made things right for myself by coming back into the highest integrity with myself so that I can continue to move forward in my life with even greater Grace, Love, Happiness and Peace in my Heart.

Since I am writing the entire story of my life in my own head and my own Heart I might as well craft a story where the Hero (me) is victorious and didn't let disappointments stop me from making my dreams come true.

Yep. That's the kind of story that I want to live.

These are my "Make lemonade out of lemons" "Pressure makes diamonds" "Out of the turd comes the Lotus" Pants.

For me, clothing is not just something that I wear. Clothing has meaning to me. The clothes that I wear are infused with symbology, energy and intention.

The Peruvian blanket is vintage and represents my deep devotion to having reverence and respect for the deep Shamanistic traditions of Peru.

The bell-bottom design represents the '70s when I was born and the freedom that has been given to me to live my life in integrity with who I am and why I am here by those who have walked the path before me.

And I made them so they are also brand-new . . . just like my eternal Soul that can emerge from any experience with renewed devotion to being a living Master of my truest, deepest and highest Self.

These pants are made out of a rainbow colored Peruvian blanket . . .

They are my "Out of the shit storm comes a rainbow" pants . . .

And they help me to deal with anything that comes my way with a sway to my hips in a ring my bell beauty giver kind of way that brings a big ole smile to my lips and encourages me to keep on walkin' with an open and authentic heart no matter what I encounter along the way. . . .

And ain't nothin' gonna break my stride.

THE POWER OF GUIDED MEDITATION

Guided Meditation and Visualization is VERY powerful.

One of my pregnant clients and friends who was a first time Mama Bird had a session scheduled on her due date but was showing absolutely no signs of labor.

We had had weekly sessions during her entire pregnancy, helping her and her in utero daughter communicate with each other so that they would feel a deep and conscious bond with each other.

During her pregnancy, my client, her daughter and I had a special familiarity and connection with each other.

At the beginning of her session on her due date she asked me to do a Guided Meditation to help her and her daughter during labor and delivery (whenever it naturally happened).

I led them both on a Guided Meditation that I created in the moment, where I was guiding them both to connect to the love, support, grounding energy and safety of the Earth, the spiritual energy, light and freedom of the Sky while describing my client's cervix gently, slowly and naturally opening like a blossom and her daughter gently, slowly and naturally dropping down toward her Mama's cervix.

It was a short meditation, maybe ten minutes long and, during it, I could feel my client's cervix gently opening and I could actually feel her daughter slowly dropping (as if it was happening inside me).

Within hours my client texted me to let me know that during our meditation the early signs of labor had started . . . some liquid had started to release from her womb so she went straight to the hospital where her water broke and she went into labor.

Eighteen hours after our session was complete her daughter was born.

WOW.

Guided Meditation and Visualization is VERY powerful.

Imagine what you could birth if you used Guided Meditation and Visualization to envision your dreams, wishes and deepest intentions.

RESISTANCE

Resistant.

It's a funny way to start describing the splendor that I experienced while on one of my South American journeys, when I felt so incredibly blessed by that incredible opportunity, but that's exactly how I felt.

Resistance.

The morning we were heading for Bolivia to go to the Island of the Sun and the Island of the Moon I felt resistant.

The seven plus hours of three vans and a boat ride across Lake Titikaka, crossing the Bolivian border, having to go through the Peruvian and Bolivian immigration process, having to pay a super high Visa fee with money that I could have used to buy several totally awesome ponchos in Peru and staying on a super rustic island that was freezing at night with no hot water or heat while some of us had tummy aches (myself included) or were raked over the coals exhausted did not sound very alluring.

But when I heard that the first and oldest Incan Temple in the world is on the Island of the Sun, I rallied because I could feel that out of the little pressures would come some mighty fine diamonds.

And I am SO happy that I didn't let my resistance and some slight discomforts stop me because I would have missed out on the awe inspiring spectacular natural beauty of Pacha Mama, incredible spiritual teachings, amazing insights, clarity and up-levelings in my consciousness, epiphanies and AHAs, deep Soul stirring remembrances of wisdom that resides at the center of my heart, business breakthroughs, unexpected gifts and a lot of laughs, sweetness and connection.

I find that sometimes when I am feeling resistant it's because I am about to go through a big portal that takes me out of my old comfortable way of being and into a new way of being that is more deeply aligned with who I truly am.

It's funny...before I came on this continuing epic initiation into my ever deepening remembrance of Andean Shamanism I was affectionately calling one of my dear hearts "Señor Resitante" (Mr. Resistant) whenever he was hitting his own resistance to growing, learning and evolving. Using the fine art and practice of humor to deal with the slight discomfort that resistance delivers made it easier for us both to navigate the resistance.

When I was happily hiking all over The Island of the Sun in total awe of everything I was witnessing, I was affectionately calling the part of myself that had been doubting the journey "Señorita Resistante" and giggling to myself about my own resistance to going out of my own comfort zone into new territory and it brought me back to innocence and humility.

Humble Innocence.

The Great Medicine for Resistance.

Oh, and Laughter too . . . because it's kinda funny how much we can all resist our own Soul's deep desire to continually transform, transmute, grow, evolve and expand.

Giving the different parts of myself (especially the troublemakers) little pet names helps bring a lot of truthful levity to my humanity.

So . . .

Buenos Dias Señor / Señora / Señorita Resistante!

I am visioning us all tapping into the superpowers of being humble and innocent today and doing our best to see the humor in life's adventurous unfolding.

And lots of love, compassion and flexibility always.

WHAT THE HUMMINGBIRD TOLD ME

As of 2017, I had taught over 23,000 hours of Yoga and had been teaching for twenty-two years and experienced something while teaching Restorative Yoga that I had never experienced before.

One of my students fell asleep in a deep relaxation Restorative Pose and began to talk in her sleep.

What she said was very clear and very bright.

She was praying for all of her family and friends.

As she spoke, so much love filled our already love filled Yoga class.

It was so beautiful and I was so touched that tears started flowing down my face.

This morning I saw a hummingbird that had a color that I have never seen before and the hummingbird told me,

"Today you are going to experience other magical things that you have never experienced before so be open and be aware."

Isn't it amazing that no matter how long we have lived and no matter how long we have done something that we can experience this day and this moment with an open heart and an open mind and allow the Great Mystery to show us something new?

For this, I am eternally and gratefully in awe.

REMEMBER TO BREATHE

Now here is some happy news:

I did a session one time with a twenty-three-year-old young man who was experiencing periodic anxiety, especially when flying.

I asked him if he was open to me teaching him some simple breath work practices and he said yes.

After a few minutes of being guided through a conscious breath work practice he told me that he felt more peaceful than he has felt in a long time.

A few days after I received a message from him telling me that he was pleased to let me know that his recent three-hour flight was the most peaceful he has ever had.

Here it is, right under our noses, or flowing through our noses . . . one of the most powerful tools for greater health, peace and happiness . . . we have 24/7 access to an incredible superpower . . . and it's free.

Remember to BREATHE.

THANKS FOR THE MAMMARIES

My Mama Bird and I were having Mother's Day Brunch one time listening to Rod Stewart sing "Thanks for the Memories" and I was singing a special Mother's Day version of the song for her:

THANKS FOR THE MAMMARIES.

I am so grateful that I was breastfed from the time I was born.

Despite the fact that no one in my Mama Bird's peer group was breastfeeding, my Mama Bird, the trailblazer, gave me the Nectar of the Goddess.

Despite the fact that someone once called her a cow (Boo!), she gave me the ultimate gift of her heart.

She knew breast milk was the very best thing for her baby girl.

I am so grateful that she had the guts, wisdom and love to give me the gift of love and high vibe life-force energy from the beginning of this magical and miraculous life.

Thanks for the mammaries Mama Bird.

ANSWERED PRAYERS

One day not long ago, a lifelong dream came true.

There is a magical Hot Springs that I have been visiting since childhood.

For many Moons I have had a deep connection to this sacred valley brimming with miraculous healing waters filled with life-giving minerals.

Every time I have been to the Hot Springs, until one special day, I have always experienced some level of sadness.

In this sacred place, I have experienced many people being rowdy, noisy, drinking beer and throwing their cans and bottles all over the place, littering and paying little or no respect to Mother Nature and the beauty of her offerings.

EVERY time I have gone there, I have prayed and I have held the vision that one day things would change.

And now, MY PRAYERS HAVE BEEN ANSWERED.

For the first time in my life I saw and felt the full manifestation of what I have been Visioning for my entire life.

Not so long ago the land was bought, is now privately owned and is now being tended by people who truly care about the magnificent Heaven on Earth that it is.

I have met one of the owners several times and two of my favorite dear hearts in the world are looking after the place. The tribe of people that are caretaking the land and waters have poured themselves into healing the land and water and have greatly raised the vibration of this magnificent place.

My heart is filled with gratitude for everything they have, are and will continue to do.

On that special day when I visited and learned and felt and saw that everything had positively changed, we soaked in the rain in the pool where the Chumash came to birth their babies.

I always feel reborn when I soak in Hot Springs and on that day I was celebrating the rebirth of those magical springs.

I am reminded that sometimes our Visions take a while to manifest but with clear intent, prayer and action POSITIVE CHANGE DOES HAPPEN eventually.

Let's all keep up the good work —> It's working.

THE GREATER PURPOSE OF PAIN

I constantly realize that one of the greatest benefits about some of the big challenges I have gone through in the past is that when I am in the presence of someone who is going through similar challenges now, I know what to say and I know what to do to love, comfort and support them.

Remember that.

Any challenges that you are going through right now will one day greatly help someone in the future.

There is a much greater purpose to everything you are facing right now.

One day it will help you to love and to serve and you will feel grateful for everything that you went through.

Honor your challenges and they will become your allies.

155

EVERYTHING IS A MIRACLE

You have never been here before.

You have never walked this path before.

You have never met the person, place or thing that stands before you now.

Since the last time you encountered whatever seems so very familiar to you, they have swapped prana, mana and mojo with an infinite number of spiraling stars, 7 billion living, breathing beings and countless expressions of the magnificent Source from which everything is born, returns to and is reborn again over and over again.

So before you project the past on this once in a lifetime moment, remember to stop, take a deep breath and remember . . .

You are in the presence of a mysterious miracle that has never been before and will never be again.

When you are fully present you will realize that right now wherever you are and whoever you are with is a magical being of ever unfolding pure potential.

This moment is the greatest adventure of your life.

RANDOM ACT OF KINDNESS

Every day can be a powerful day.

One day I started the day with a commitment to do
a random act of kindness for a stranger.

I had no idea what that might be but I knew that the
opportunity would present itself.

First thing, I went to my mechanic because a warning light
had come on in my Toyota Prius.

After they inspected my car, I learned that I needed a new
battery that was going to be a very unexpected big expense.

It was then that I knew that my random act of kindness
would have something to do with giving someone money.

Because today giving money would be more of a stretch
than most days when I don't have a big unexpected
expense in my life.

I regularly give money to charities that I support, give
money to homeless people and have given money to
many people who I believe in.

I recalled a story that Tony Robbins once told about a time
when he had about twenty-five dollars left to his name and

paid for someone's meal at a restaurant in the spirit of trust in the Universe and in the spirit of giving, graciousness and Universal Love.

He says that was the moment that his entire life turned around and that was the moment when he became a truly wealthy man.

He said it was the best day of his life.

Shortly after leaving my mechanic I stopped by Trader Joe's and lots of magical things happen for me in Trader Joe's and today was one of the most magical days ever.

Within a few minutes, while I was in the produce area, I overheard a man saying out loud:

I AM THE MASTER OF MY FATE.
I AM THE CAPTAIN OF MY SOUL

And he continued to walk around the produce area, cheese section and nut and dried fruit section saying the entire Invictus poem by William Ernest Henley.

This was not a crazy man.

He was an eighty-something-year-old man grocery shopping with his wife while reciting poetry.

He was truly self-possessed, sovereign and so present.

He was talking about what truly matters.

He was a Divine Messenger.

And I was paying attention.

We locked eyes and I smiled at him with deep acknowledgment as he walked around and he said again,

"I AM THE MASTER OF MY FATE. I AM THE CAPTAIN OF MY SOUL."

I walked up to him, said, "Thank You" and gave him a big hug to which he replied with a giant smile,

"Well, if walking around Trader Joe's reciting poetry is going to get me great hugs like that one, then I am going to do it more often."

Shortly thereafter synchronicity brought us together at the cash register at the same moment.

I asked my checkout man to hand a twenty-dollar bill to Poetry Man's checkout man to apply the twenty dollars to his bill.

My checkout man gave me a big ole Namaste with his hands and said,

"Thank You!"

He had a giant smile on his face.

Poetry Man had no idea that I had given his checkout man the twenty-dollar bill.

And his checkout man did not tell him that I had given him the twenty dollars. He just subtracted twenty dollars from his bill.

And then I overheard Poetry Man saying,

"Is my bill over thirty dollars? Because if it is I need to put some things back. We don't have more than thirty dollars to spend."

The checkout man said,

"You're all good, Sir."

I was tearing up on the way back to my car because I was so happy.

Acts of Random Kindness truly do make us feel happy.

I gave to someone who gave to me.

He gave me inspiration. And he inspired me to give.

And I really needed what he gave me. And he really needed what I gave him.

The best thing is how much I received that day by giving.

Pay it forward.

Let me know about how giving makes you feel more happy.

I feel it's important for us to share these stories with each other because they have the ability to uplift, inspire and motivate us and increase our faith and trust in the goodness of life.

MEDITATION IS THE SHIT

I have a wonderful client who was a first time Mama Bird with a newborn baby.

We did sessions every week during her pregnancy and I supported her as she developed a deep relationship with her baby en utero. We always included her daughter in our sessions, discussions and meditations.

When her daughter was born, her daughter instantly recognized my voice because she had heard it once a week when she was in the womb.

Recently the baby girl was having some troubles with her digestion and elimination and had not taken a poop for a week.

So sad.

So I made a special Guided Meditation for her to support her in relaxing and releasing.

I spoke with her Mama Bird yesterday.

She told me that she lay down with her newborn daughter earlier in the day and they listened to the meditation together.

Shortly thereafter her daughter took her first poop in a week. Yay!

Meditation is super powerful.

Meditation can help you "let that shit go" literally and metaphorically.

Clearly, MEDITATION IS THE SHIT.

ANYTHING HELPS

I was driving to meet a friend for a hike at dawn, I was playing a song that I really love really loud and was singing and dancing in my car.

When I exited the freeway and pulled up to the stop sign, there was a man standing at the corner with a sign that said,

HUNGRY. ANYTHING HELPS.

I thought, if anything helps,

Maybe he is hungry for a laugh.

Maybe he is hungry for a song and dance.

So I rolled down my window and started singing for him.

And maybe he was hungry for some food.

So I gave him some money.

And maybe he was hungry for love.

So I told him "I love you."

UNWAVERING FAITH

I have a wonderful friend.

Synchronicity brought us together in a magical way.

His name is Brian and he lives in England and is seventy-three years old.

As it turns out he has the exact same birthday as my Dad who passed away when I was twenty-eight and he was fifty-six.

Since my Dad passed, I have always felt my Dad's presence around me and have always felt that he is one of my Guardian Angels. Now I feel I have an Earth Angel in my new friend.

One morning he was telling me that a couple of years ago he had gone through a challenging emotional situation and that during that time he was struck with a stabbing pain in his chest.

After a few hours of dealing with the pain he called a friend to ask for help and his friend called the paramedics.

When the paramedics arrived they hooked him up to an EKG and told him that he had been having a heart attack for three hours! They said that they had never seen or heard of such a thing and were shocked that he was standing, talking or even alive.

When they looked at his ID and found out he was in his seventies they were even more shocked and told him that despite having a heart attack that he had the physiology of a forty-eight year old man.

I asked him what he feels is his secret to surviving the heart attack and to longevity and he said,

"UNWAVERING FAITH IN GOD."

He asked me if I had ever heard of the poem "Footsteps in the Sand" by Mary Stevenson and then he recited it to me:

"One night I dreamed a dream. As I was walking along the beach with my Lord. Across the dark sky flashed scenes from my life. For each scene, I noticed two sets of footprints in the sand, One belonging to me and one to my Lord.

After the last scene of my life flashed before me, I looked back at the footprints in the sand. I noticed that at many times along the path of my life, especially at the very lowest and saddest times, there was only one set of footprints.

This really troubled me, so I asked the Lord about it.

'Lord, you said once I decided to follow you, You'd walk with me all the way. But I noticed that during the saddest and most troublesome times of my life, there was only one set of footprints. I don't understand why, when I needed You the most, You would leave me.'

He whispered,

'My precious child, I love you and will never leave you. Never, ever, during your trials and testings. When you saw only one set of footprints, It was then that I carried you.'"

I told him I have always loved that poem.

Then I told him about one of my very favorite comic strips that has a picture of "God" and a man.

God says,

"My child, I never left you. Those places with one set of footprints? It was then that I carried you. That long groove over there is when I dragged you for a while."

We laughed hysterically and uncontrollably for about a minute.

After all, FAITH IN GOD and LAUGHTER are two of the greatest keys to a long, happy and healthy life.

So are Guardian Angels.

Keep the Faith and keep Laughing sweet ones and be on the lookout for your Guardian Angels —> They are everywhere.

PERPETUAL ORGASM

Oh, the wondrous conversations that I am a part of at the Esalen Institute . . .

I was teaching there once and it was the last day of a Tantra workshop. At breakfast one of the participants was talking about his eight-hour-long
PERPETUAL ORGASM.

Let's imagine the possibilities . . .

For me, the art and practice of Tantra is summed up as
If anything is sacred, then everything is sacred.
Or,
Everyday Enlightenment.
Tantra is far more than just sex.

Imagine if we walked around for most of our day feeling connected to all of existence, in a heightened state of reverence for all of life's unfolding, grateful for every experience and every breath, feeling love for every moment.
That is bliss.
That is orgasm.

Today my intention is to have a PERPETUAL ORGASM.
Care to join me?

THE CHEER IS HERE

I had an entire week of work that was perpetually so incredibly sweet and touching . . .

At the end of nearly every class I have taught and session I facilitated, all of the people that I was working with clapped and cheered.

The reason that this is so lovely for me is that it demonstrates at a core level that these incredible adults have retained their childlike sense of innocence, celebration, wonder and appreciation.

It's a beautiful indication that they are all connected with their essence.

And I am clapping and cheering for us all to do the same.

THE CHURCH OF TRADER JOE'S

The Church of Trader Joe's did it again.

One night in the checkout line, I asked my wonderful cashier, "How are you?"

He said,

"I am doing well . . . just doing my best to help out all the folks that are displaced and staying in hotels after the mudslide."

I said,

"Thank you for everything you are doing for our wonderful community."

He said,

"It is my pleasure.
How are you doing after the mudslide?"

I said,

"Well, we lost my childhood home where my Mama Bird lived, but my Mom, brother in law, niece and nephew were rescued by the National Guard and made it out and my family and I are counting our blessings and we are simply grateful for the miracle that they are still alive and not hurt."

He said,

"I am so sorry for your loss.

Wait just a minute.

I will be right back."

He came back with a bouquet of flowers and said,

"Please give these flowers to your Mama and tell her how sorry we are for her loss and that Trader Joe's loves her."

HOW TO CREATE CONNECTION AND EXPERIENCE EVERYDAY INITIATIONS

Now you know about some of the sweet connections and everyday initiations that I have experienced and I hope it inspires you to create more connection in your daily life and to experience the everyday spiritual initiations that are always available to you everywhere all the time.

But how?

I have created a "how to" framework for you to consider, practice and apply in your own life if it resonates with you.

If it resonates with you and you find it helpful, then please share this framework with your loved ones.

I have made the guidelines very simple.

They are simple, but they are not always easy to practice.

The trick after being inspired about anything is to maintain the inspirational turning point that you experienced in your consciousness by practicing what you have learned.

Practicing these five steps daily is the key to embodying them so that your mere presence attracts wonderful interactions and initiations. The five steps to experiencing more connection and everyday initiations are:

1. Be yourself and love yourself.
2. You are a powerful creator.
3. Don't be indifferent; make a difference.
4. Make kindness your Religion.
5. Be the change you want to see in the world.

Step 1: Be yourself and love yourself

The wisdom of all world cultures, religions and spiritual traditions suggest that the microcosm reflects the macrocosm and the macrocosm reflects the microcosm.

As within so without.

As above so below.

Whatever is happening inside will be reflected outside.

Whatever is happening outside will be reflected inside.

The core teaching of Yoga and many other ancient traditions is unity consciousness.

Even science has proven that everything in existence is connected.

Basically, there is no escaping connection.

So you might as well make peace with the fact that you are connected to every person, place and thing in your presence.

Even the people, places and things you wish you were not connected to.

Damn.

Them too?

Yep.

Them too.

We are hardwired for connection.

Connection starts inside you.

Your body, mind, heart, Soul and Spirit working together as a unified team.

Once you feel harmonious internal connection it's a lot easier to experience harmony with the people, places and things around you.

When you were born, you were a bright shining Soul.

But there is an innate problem that your Soul has probably faced at some point in your life.

In some small or perhaps big way, you have disconnected from who you truly are, what is most important to you and why you are here.

The main way this happens is that you started taking on a bunch of beliefs, ideas, thoughts, emotions, actions and ways of being and doing that are not aligned with your true self.

You took on some "not self" energy from the people, places and things around you.

Of course it began when you were a child.

You were taught ideas about what is right and wrong.

You were taught about how you should think, feel, believe and act.

Your survival depended on being loved and accepted by your parents, family and caretakers.

In some way you made some wise decisions (at the time) to align with and take on your parents', family's and caretakers' way of being and doing so that you would be loved and accepted and would have your baseline needs and your emotional needs met.

Even if you felt like, or deep down inside knew, that their way of being and doing wasn't a total match for you, you might have taken on some of that "not your true self" energy to fit in and be loved.

Examples of taking on "not self" family of origin energy that doesn't truly resonate with you are:

Eating like your family eats even though it makes you feel awful.

Going to your family's church even though you don't feel the presence of the God or Creator of your understanding there or don't believe in God at all.

Carrying on the family business even though it doesn't feel truly purposeful or meaningful to you personally.

Or it can be more subtle, such as:

Repeating negative patterns your parents have made in relationships, finances or career and you end up feeling like "Oh my God! I am turning into my Mother/Father/Grandfather/Grandmother, etc." It's almost like a little mask, disguise or camouflage that you wore. Unless you were raised by parents and family who 100 percent wanted you to be exactly who you are, then you probably have some very subtle or perhaps very obvious layers of other people's energy covering up your true essence.

It can then, of course, extend out beyond your family of origin to society.

Society has projected a lot onto you about how you should be. You may have taken on some of society's projections that are not aligned with your true blueprint so that you will fit in and won't be kicked out of your tribe.

Societal projections of what you should be/accomplish are things like:

You should go to college and get a degree in four years.

You should get a nine-to-five job straight out of college with a regular paycheck, benefits and a retirement plan.

You should get married by the time you are twenty-five

You should buy a house with a white picket fence.

You should have two kids.

Maybe these familial and societal expectations are aligned with who you truly are and what is truly important to you.

If that's the case, then awesome!

If you have taken on some of this "not self" energy that isn't aligned for you, then it might serve you well to investigate why you have done so.

The reason you took on this "not self" energy is usually based in fear.

Fear of not being loved.

Fear of rejection.

Fear of failure.

When you are afraid you don't feel safe. So you played it safe by taking on these "not self" ways of operating so that you will be loved, feel connected and belong.

If you hide your true beliefs, your true purpose, your true values, your true desires and your true vision for yourself and your life, then you have given into some false power that you feel will make everything okay because you are not rocking the boat of what is considered normal.

But what you end up with is not true love.

It's not true connection.

And it is not true belonging.

If you allow yourself to be controlled by the illusion that, if you do what you are "supposed" to do, there will be safety, order, peace and harmony in your family and in your society, you might just feel the exact opposite.

In actuality, doing what you are "supposed" to do if it is not aligned with who you truly are, will definitely not create a true sense of safety, order, peace and harmony.

In fact it can create depression and desperation if you suppress your true nature because in truth being who you truly are is the greatest gift you can give yourself and the world.

You can end up feeling trapped in a system that you don't even believe in, overloaded with responsibilities that are not even truly meaningful to you.

You can end up feeling very angry and resentful if you give up your dreams and give your power away to a family or societal system that is not supportive of you actualizing your highest potential and greatest visions.

Of course, you are doing everything you can to stay aligned with your truest, deepest and highest self at the level of consciousness that you have.

If you feel like none of the above has ever applied to you, then CONGRATULATIONS! You have managed to stay true to you, the greatest victory that one can accomplish in a world that so often tries to convince you to be anything other than who you truly are.

One way or another, the challenge you will sometimes face by staying attuned to your essence is that some people will judge you and some will resent you and you will trigger some people because if you can stay connected to your true self that means that they can do it too.

If they are feeling trapped in a cocoon of "not self" energy, then freeing yourself can piss them off or make them feel jealous because they actually want what you have

Sadly, that is not a true family member or friend.

However, if you can maintain your essence, then you will ultimately experience incredible freedom, contentment and inner harmony.

As long as you are not harming anyone and being a tyrant or menace to your family or society, then please stay true to yourself.

If you do not maintain your essence and allow your essence to be corrupted, you will experience major internal chaos.

Not staying connected to your essence creates chaos in your innate nature because each of us is hardwired for truth and authenticity. If you are not being who you truly are, then you are not going to experience true connection with others.

If you have corrupted your true nature to fit in with your family and tribe, then the opposite will happen: you will experience chaos with your family and chaos with your tribe because you are essentially trapped in illusions.

And illusions are not sustainable.

They eventually crumble.

But who is your true family and who is your true tribe?

Hopefully your true family is your blood relatives.

Hopefully your true tribe is the society in which you live.

But sometimes your true family is not your blood family or at least some of the members of your blood family are not your true family.

Sometimes your true family is what I call your Soul family made up of the amazing friends who truly love and support you and who you truly love and support.

Sometimes your true society might be found in an alternative community or another country than the one you were raised in.

These relationships and connections are based in the mutual energy of wanting each other to realize and fully embody our truest, deepest and highest sense of self.

I was the one who coined the phrase:

Your vibe attracts your tribe.

It went viral because it's true.

The highest vibe you can possibly tap into is you being who you truly are.

When you take off the "not self" mask, fully embrace and live in integrity with your true self and let your Soul shine, you will become incredibly radiant and attractive.

And your radiant light is what attracts your true tribe.

So be yourself and love yourself.

How do you love yourself?

Take care of yourself.

How do you take care of yourself?

Everyday,

Stay connected to your higher purpose.

Stay connected to your true values.

Stay connected to your dreams and your visions.

Eat healthful food that makes you feel nourished.

Move your body so you stay strong, flexible and balanced.

Consciously breathe to clear stress and tension and to reoxygenate and energize yourself.

Meditate. Be still. Go within. Cultivate inner peace.

Pray and ask for love, support and guidance from your truest, deepest and highest self and the God/Goddess/ Benevolent Force of your personal understanding.

Cleanse your physical body of toxins and impurities.

Cleanse your heart and emotional body of stress and heavy energy.

Rest and relax and sleep deeply.

Consciously surround yourself with people who truly love and support you and who you truly love and support.

Be grateful and focus on the countless blessings in your life.

This is the baseline of staying connected to your true self and loving yourself.

Of course there is more to it, but this is the foundation.

These foundations make you feel really good and really comfortable in your own skin.

They make you like yourself and love yourself.

And then anywhere you go you feel comfortable and at home with yourself.

Anywhere you go, even if you are by yourself, you will feel like you are on an adventure with your best friend and a hot date with the most amazing love in existence.

This foundation of cultivating your true self through daily self-love and self-care creates inner connectedness between your body, mind, heart, Soul and Spirit and will attract to you, beautiful connections and will prepare you to show up as your higher self in the everyday initiations that will come your way.

So, be yourself and love yourself.

You have to be intimate with yourself first and foremost before you can create intimacy with others.

You have to know yourself and be yourself in order to truly know others and be with others.

If you are not in balance, then none of your other relationships with people, places and things will be in balance.

Be 100 percent yourself so that everyone in your presence feels 100 percent safe, loved and supported in being their 100 percent selves too.

This creates a very clean and clear energetic in the world where nothing is hidden and there are no false fronts.

This is the key to creating internal and external connection and harmony and true order inside and all around us in the world.

It all begins with you being you and loving yourself just as you truly are.

Then your mere presence will inspire others to do and be the same. You being truly you and loving who you truly are and loving and supporting everyone and everything in your presence in being and doing the same is the ultimate everyday initiation.

Step 2: You are a powerful creator.

Did you know that there are studies about your personal impact on the world?

There is an incredible Institute called HeartMath that studies the power of the heart and its impact on the people, places and things around us.

HeartMath has scientifically proven the amazing and vital role of the heart in our lives, and how our personal energy impacts our relationships with others and ultimately affects the consciousness of the world.

Your energy, which is your core superpower, is not a fantasy! Your superpowers are backed by science!

Scientists have proven and Spiritualists know from experience: Whatever energy you are feeling and embodying is being broadcast out into the world and affects everyone and everything in your presence.

Whether or not you like it, your vibe not only attracts your tribe, your vibe affects your tribe.

If you feel negative emotions and you are not processing them and they are cesspooling inside you, then you are going to negatively impact the world around you.

Have you ever stepped in dog pooh and didn't realize it and, everywhere you go, you smell pooh and think it's someone else until someone else says,

"Did you know you stepped in pooh? It smells really bad."

That is how unprocessed negative emotions inside you are.

You can't cover that pooh up.

Everyone can smell it.

Vibes are like a smell.

You can't necessarily see them, but you can definitely sense them.

And science has proven it.

If you have positive emotions and you are consciously generating more of them and they are powerfully building inside you, then you are going to positively impact the world around you.

Have you ever been in line at the grocery store and had a sweet and simple interaction with the checkout person and they say,

"You just made my day! Who are you?"

That is how incredibly powerful you are.

And my gut tells me that you have been underestimating just how powerful you are and what a huge impact you have on the world around you.

So how do you cultivate your superpowers as a creator of good vibes in the world?

You have to be very intentional about your mission here on Planet Earth.

I believe that when you were born you knew who you truly were and why you are truly here.

You have a higher purpose.

So first of all you need to know what your higher purpose is and intentionally live in alignment with it every day.

And I sure hope that, when you discover it or remember it, that it inspires you and motivates you to want to be a powerful creator of good vibes in the world.

When I say your purpose I am not talking about your job, although hopefully your job is aligned with your higher purpose.

Your higher purpose is who you are 24/7 no matter where you are or who you are with.

My higher purpose is:

I am the most benevolent extension of the Benevolent

Source everywhere all the time with everyone and everything in my presence.

Goodness gracious! That is a big higher purpose and it is really challenging to abide by it.

I fumble and stumble some days and that's why I say the Hawaiian Kahuna Prayer called Ho'o'ponopono a lot:

I love you.

I am sorry.

Please forgive me.

Thank you.

That helps to clear the air so that the powerful light of my higher purpose can prevail again.

You have to remind yourself of your higher purpose every day and some days you have to remind yourself of who you truly are and why you are truly here several times throughout the day.

When you are going through a big challenge in life, which we all do, I recommend setting a timer to go off once every hour to remind yourself of your higher purpose.

It is really easy to forget who you are and why you're here.

It's easy to go off course and in fact we all go off course, sometimes just a little and sometimes a lot.

Even if you know your purpose, there might come a day when you realize:

What the heck happened?

How did I get here?

I am out of alignment with my higher purpose right now.

Here is the deal:

Life is going to challenge you every day.

Do you think it's easy to be the most benevolent extension of the Benevolent Source in every moment on every day?

No.

It is full on Advanced True Self Mastery to stay aligned with and be the living embodiment of your higher purpose.

Every day something challenging can happen to you and your ego, your little self will say to you,

"You can live in alignment with your higher purpose most days, but not now because that person is being a total jerk so you should be a total jerk too. It's only fair."

As Gandhi said,

"An eye for an eye makes the whole world blind."

So you have to train yourself to be yourself.

Like an athlete you have to train yourself to stay aligned with your higher purpose and to continuously be a powerful creator of the good stuff and not the pooh stuff.

You have to remind yourself that you are a powerful creator of your own experiences in the world and take personal responsibility for your life and what happens.

I know it's a hard pill to swallow, but it's the truth and it is truly empowering to get back in the driver's seat and consciously steer your life in the direction that your true self wants to go and do it with clarity and intention.

So get clear about the energy that you want to create in the world. Then practice it everywhere and with everyone.

This is how you stay connected to your true self and create connection with those in your presence.

Every day and everywhere you flow continuously initiates you into the art and practice of staying connected to your essence and your higher purpose.

Your life is your work of art.

Every moment is an initiation of staying true to you and your higher purpose.

No matter what happens.

Choose and claim to make every moment a powerful and beautiful creation.

Step 3: Don't be indifferent; make a difference.

There is a powerful quote by a Holocaust survivor named Elie Wiesel that perfectly sums up this step:

"The opposite of love is not hate, it's indifference.

The opposite of art is not ugliness, it's indifference.

The opposite of faith is not heresy, it's indifference.

The opposite of life is not death, it's indifference."

Indifference is when you don't care, are not concerned, are apathetic about and are overly detached from life and living and/or the world's many challenges and problems . . . especially when they are not yours.

It is when you think that the world's problems are so huge that there is nothing that you can do to truly help and move the needle in a positive direction. It is when you say,

"I'm not going to do anything because it won't make a difference anyway."

If you have ever felt that way or feel that way now, I feel you.

The energy of indifference is an epidemic on Planet Earth.

We can all feel it. You can feel the jostled energy in the air. You are sensitive. You are empathic. You are compassionate. You feel the stress, tension, pain and discomfort that the world feels. You feel it all because you have a big heart and you love and care deeply. I know it can all feel so overwhelming and even unbearable at times.

When things get challenging in the world around you, have you ever asked yourself,

"How the heck could these things be happening?

What the heck is going on?

What has the world come to?

Really?

Is this for real?

Is this really happening?"

At those times I know you've probably questioned whether your love, light and leadership is even making a true difference in a big way. In those times, maybe you have even wanted to hide out or numb out or hit the road. You might feel indifferent and want to throw in the towel because your vision for what you've always dreamed is possible for our planet seems so far away.

Indifference is when you see a homeless person asking for money and you pretend not to see them or turn away when they speak to you instead of acknowledging them and saying,

"Here is a dollar"

or

"I'm sorry I don't have any change but I wish you all the best."

It's when you see an elderly person struggling to open the door and you don't help them because you're in a rush rather than taking an extra minute to hold the door open and say,

"There you go. Have a nice day."

It's when your loved one is sick and you don't reach out to them because you are so busy when you could take just one minute to send a simple text that says,

"I heard you are not feeling well. I am so sorry. Is there anything I can bring you? I am sending you healing energy."

It's when there is an earthquake or flood or fire or mudslide in your community and you feel too overwhelmed with sadness about it so you don't do anything to help rather than reaching out to those in need to give them shelter, a warm meal, money, clothing, a hug or a consoling conversation.

As you know, the world's problems are not getting any better right now.

As long as anyone stays indifferent about the world's problems, the world's problems are not going to be solved.

In those moments when you feel overwhelmed and become indifferent because you don't think your help will make a difference, please don't stop. Please don't give up. Please don't lose your faith.

Dr. Martin Luther King Jr. said,

"It is not just the vitriolic words and violent actions of bad people that are responsible for where we are as a country. It's also the appalling silence and inaction of good people."

Remember that just one small step in the right direction will keep you on the right path and will help that person, that place or that thing.

Dr. Martin Luther King Jr. had some wise words about that as well: "The journey of a thousand miles begins with one step."

What is one thing that you can do right now and every day that you know always makes you feel better?

Take a walk.

Take ten deep breaths.

Write down three things that you are grateful for.

Do something to keep your energy flowing rather than stagnating and getting stuck.

Mother Teresa said,

"Not all of us can do great things. But we can do small things with great love."

What is one thing you can do or say right now and every day that will make someone else feel better?

Reach out to a friend and ask them to have tea.

Give 10 percent of whatever you earn to a charity that you believe in.

Tell your lover, friend or relative three things that you appreciate about them.

Say hello to a stranger.

Compliment your waitress on her beautiful sweater.

Volunteer for an organization that you feel is doing good work in the world.

Help.

Keep moving.

Keep breathing.

Keep loving.

Keep doing something.

Anything.

Everything counts and everything helps.

But please don't do nothing.

And keep making wise choices for yourself moment by moment to keep yourself inspired, enthusiastic and motivated.

Read inspirational stories about inspirational people doing inspirational things.

Even if you don't believe it truly makes a difference, at the end of the day at least you will feel like you did your best to be the best that you could be and to make a positive contribution in the world.

Please don't be indifferent.

Make a difference.

YOU make a difference.

When you make a difference it makes you different.

It makes you special.

So many people are letting indifference stop them.

When you take responsibility for being the one who can consciously shift the energy of any situation it makes you different.

It makes you unique.

Because it is rare.

When you are the first one to smile at a stranger.

When you ask a stranger:

How are you?

When you open the door, pay a compliment, volunteer your time, people will feel that you are different.

You aren't just thinking about you.

You are thinking about everyone and how you and your energy, your thoughts and emotions and your actions impact everyone around you.

When people are in your presence, they will feel warmth and love and true caring.

Most people will be inspired by you and will want to carry forth that energy into the rest of their day.

They too will want to be different by not being indifferent and making a difference.

Every moment is your initiation out of indifference and into making a difference.

And that is how we can positively transform the world one person and one everyday initiation at a time.

Step 4: Make kindness your Religion

Some of the greatest spiritual teachers and leaders in the world said that kindness is the ultimate path in this life.

The Dalai Lama said,

"My religion is very simple. My religion is kindness."

Mother Teresa had a lot to say about kindness and love:

"Peace begins with a smile."

Kind words can be short and easy to speak, but their echoes are truly endless.

Let no one ever come to you without leaving better and happier.

Be the living expression of God's kindness: kindness in your face, kindness in your eyes, kindness in your smile.

And then there is the good ole bumper sticker that we have all seen many times that says:
COMMIT RANDOM ACTS OF KINDNESS AND SENSELESS BEAUTY.

We have all been conditioned to think that spirituality requires some special ceremony or initiation or that you have to go someplace special like a church or temple to have a spiritual experience.
Believe me!
I love going to churches and temples.
I love creating religious and spiritual ceremonies and rituals.
I have gone through many spiritual initiations.

However, spirituality can really be quite simple and is found everywhere all the time.

Some of the greatest, most down to earth, accessible to anyone anywhere religions, churches, temples, synagogues, rituals, ceremonies and initiations are the everyday initiations that we go through.
Every moment is a spiritual moment when we regard the present moment and whoever is with us as being the living embodiment of Great Spirit/God/Creator and treat everyone and everything with simple kindness.

But we make things way too complicated.
We oftentimes think God is someplace else other than right here where we are.

There is a great Greek Myth that says,

"Hide God in the Humans . . . They will never think to look there."

The question is:

Are you looking for God in the humans who are in your presence?

Whoever you are with, whether it's your parent, child, spouse, brother, sister, grocery clerk, homeless person or the person that just cut you off in traffic and then flipped you off . . . well, they are a spiritual being.

Perhaps they are an incredibly well disguised God, or spiritual being, but nevertheless they are an extension of the Benevolent Force.

You smiling, you being kind, you being just a very basic baseline gracious human being with everyone can be your very simple and very attainable religion.

Even the Bible says,

"Be kind to one another (Ephesians 4:32)."

I love the acronym "Good Orderly Direction" for G.O.D.

Being Godly is simply moving through life in the direction of what is good, kind, harmonious and orderly.

It is your ability to see through the disguise that is covering up someone's Soul.

Just because you are kind doesn't mean that everyone else is.

Sometimes people do not act kindly at all.

This is what I like to call The Advanced Course . . . remembering that everyone is a spiritual being.

Perhaps they forgot that they are a spiritual being and that might be why they are not acting kindly.

That doesn't mean that you should too.

The ultimate everyday Initiation then is:

Can you maintain your vibration of kindness no matter how someone else is treating you?

I am visioning that you can.

And it takes practice.

Be patient.

Keep practicing kindness and soon, like the Dalai Lama, kindness may become your religion too.

Step 5. Be the change you want to see in the world.

The great mystical poet Rumi said,

"Yesterday I was clever, so I wanted to change the world. Today I am wise so I am changing myself."

Michael Jackson said,

"I'm looking at the man in the mirror. I'm asking him to change his ways. And no message could have been any clearer. If you want to make the world a better place, take a look at yourself and make the change."

Jill Jackson and Sy Miller wrote a song with the lyrics

"Let there be peace on earth, and let it begin with me."

There is an epidemic in the world that creates disempowerment in us all.

The epidemic is that someone else should be the one to be kind, to take the lead, to make the change, to make a difference.

But as we can clearly see, a lot of the people in leadership positions are not leading with kindness, love, peace, unity and harmony.

A lot of the world leaders are leading with the exact opposite energy of kindness, love, peace, unity and harmony.

This can be very disempowering if you don't activate leadership within yourself and decide: I am going to be the one.

I am going to be the one to smile first.

I am going to be the one to ask a stranger:

How are you?

I am going to be the one to say something off beat and funny.

I am going to be the one to make the first move.

I am going to connect with someone right now because I want to experience more connection in the world.

Because I am a leader of kindness and love and peace and harmony.

Do not wait for leaders to take the lead and positively transform this planet.

You might be waiting a long time.

Do it yourself.

Do it alone if you must.

Start your own grassroots movement of goodness and work person to person and moment to moment.

Never worry about how many lives you are touching with your open heart.

Help one person at a time and always start with the person nearest you.

Go out into the world today and love the people you

meet. Let your presence light new light in the hearts of people.

I tell total strangers,
"I love you and I support you."
I do it all the time.

I tell people I have never met before,
"I am holding you in my heart and in my prayers."

I say these things because I know that this is what the world needs most.
I say these things because I know that this is what humans most need.
We all need to know that we are loved and that someone cares about us.
If this is what you want and this is the kind of world that you want to live in, then flow this energy into the world.

The great and ironic thing is, you will receive the blessings of whatever energy is flowing from your heart.
As you flow this energy from your heart, it will feel so good to others that your presence will initiate others into kindness, love and connection.
They will then pass it along to the next person they interact with.

And so on and so on until more and more people are flowing love, kindness and true connection from their hearts.

It all begins with you being the change that you so deeply want to see in the world.

LET'S DO THIS

The world truly needs your presence, love and goodness now more than ever.

There are so many horrible things happening in the world.

Let's be part of the good news.

Let's be cocreators of truly sweet moments of connection.

If you want to experience more powerful and positive stories and everyday initiations in your own life, here is the first thing to do right now:

Focus on the last time you felt peace, love and harmony.

Visualize where you were, what you were doing and who you were with.

Tap back into the feelings and tap back into that memory.

Let those images and feelings fill you up completely.

Recognize that, if it happened before, it can happen again and again and again.

Try saying this out loud every day before you go out and about in the world:

"From this day forward, I am going to think, feel, speak and act in alignment with my truest, deepest and highest self.

I am going to be who I truly am and I am going to love myself and take super good care of myself.

I am going to be a powerful creator and I am cocreating goodness, love, peace and connection with everyone I interact with today.

I am going to make a positive difference in this world one person at a time.

I am going to make my spiritual path very simple.

Kindness is my religion.

I am going to be the change I want to see in the world.

So be it. So it is."

And then go out into the world and see what kind of magical experiences you attract.

Once you get into the groove of it, shift up your intention a bit.

Truly energize your words with the resonance of your Soul and before you walk out the door every morning say,

"I am thinking, feeling, speaking and acting in alignment with my truest, deepest and highest self.

I am who I truly am and I love myself and take super good care of myself.

I am a powerful creator and I am cocreating goodness, love, peace and connection with everyone I interact with today.

I am making a positive difference in this world one person at a time.

I am walking a very simple spiritual path. Kindness is my religion.

I am the change I want to see in the world.

I am playing the leading role in the best story that was ever lived.

I am cocreating beautiful stories of love, connection, fun and harmony with the people that I interact with today.

So be it. So it is."

And then go out into the world and see what kind of sweet stories you cocreate with the people you attract into your day.

This might be new to you.

As the great saying goes,

Insanity is doing the same thing over and over and expecting to get a different result.

So try something new.

Try being super intentional with your day.

Set the intention of connection with others.

Then feel the joy and goodness that is coming your way.

Living this way might even feel a little scary.

As the great saying goes:

Do one thing every day that scares you.

Internal connection with yourself and external connection with others requires practice and patience.

Every day keep practicing your intentions and taking simple actions of kindness in the world.

Throughout the day, focus on all the great connections you are making and be grateful for them.

Don't focus on the connections you don't have or are not making. When you focus on the positive you will attract the positive.

Cultivate faith and trust that these stories and everyday initiations are going to happen when you are ready.

At the end of the day, celebrate all the signs of connection that you experienced.

There are two very powerful studies that are incredibly important to remember about life and living.

In one study, people were interviewed at the end of their lives about what life is all about and what is most important about life and living.

Everyone across the boards said that their relationships with others and the connections that they cultivated with their loved ones, community members and total strangers as well are the most important part of life and make life worth living.

They all wished that they had been who they truly are and had not held back their true self.

They all wished that they had not worked so hard.

They all wished that they had spent more time cultivating love and connection with others.

In another recent study people were tested about what creates true physical, mental and emotional health and longevity.

More than nutrition . . .

More than exercise . . .

More than meditation . . .

More than rest, relaxation and sleeping . . .

Connection with others is the number one thing that creates lasting health and longevity.

Isn't that amazing?!

Disconnection is one of the leading causes of sadness, depression and even suicide in our world.

Nowadays it is rare to go anywhere and see a couple or friends or a family truly connecting with each other.

Everyone is on their phones.

Yes, our phones are one of the ways we create connection with each other through texting, messaging, calling, emailing and connecting through social media.

But it is also one of the leading causes of disconnection with the actual people that are in your presence.

So if you want more true happiness, fulfillment and connection, put down your phone.

Look people in their eyes.

Have a conversation in real time.

That is the connection that your Soul is truly craving.

And you can't find it in your phone.

We humans need a sense of family and belonging.

Maybe you are not close with your family of origin but you can experience a feeling of belonging by connecting with your global family.

The more of us that flow kindness from our hearts, the greater sense of belonging and family we cultivate with everyone everywhere.

There is one more story I want to share with you about someone else I know who realized that love and connection are the most important things in life.

While writing this book, the community where I grew up in Montecito, California went through a huge tragedy.

There was a devastating mudslide that killed many people, injured many people, destroyed many homes and greatly damaged many homes.

My childhood home was destroyed in the mudslide while my Mama Bird, Brother in Law, nephew and niece were in the house.

Thank goodness they, the cat and even the three hens were not injured and survived.

They were literally stuck in the one small area of the house that was not completely filled with mud and annihilated for eight hours without power or water.

They were rescued by the National Guard and the Montecito Fire Department.

The house was totally destroyed and will be demolished.

It was possible to salvage some of the possessions in the house, but only if we went digging through the mud.

So my entire family literally dug in the mud for months and months.

I was told by the mud that if I spent time in the mud that the mud would give me many messages.

Indeed it has.

I had no idea that anything of mine was still in my childhood home. But alas, my sister found a small keepsake box of letters that were written to me while I was between eighteen to twenty-two years old. Amidst the letters was a letter from my dear ole Dad.

The huge tragedy that my family went through exactly twenty years ago was my Dad dying of Cancer when he was only fifty-six years old.

So it was very special to find the letter from him.

It is the most powerful letter he ever wrote and I will never forget the profound message that he delivered to me in it.

He wrote the letter eight years before he passed away.

In the letter he told me that my health and well-being are the most important things in life.

He also said the most important things in life are love and the relationships and connections that we create with family and loved ones.

He said he wished that he hadn't worked so hard.

He said working so hard was his way of providing for our family, but that it also took some time away from spending quality time with us. He said he wished he had learned this earlier in life.

He said he hoped that I apply these things to my own life

He died eight years after writing the letter.

A week before he died he told me that if he had to walk this path of life all over again that he would walk the path that I am on.

He was talking about everything that I have shared with you in this book.

I pass his message and my message on to you today with a vision that you will take it to heart.

If you are working too hard and not taking enough time to connect with your loved ones and the people that you encounter every day, then please consider a course correction.

The correction is connection.

Stop waiting.

Now is the only moment to live and love and every moment is the most important and valuable moment of your life.

Your future life is being created right now.

And right now in this moment is the best time ever to let your guard down and truly live and truly love.

Every situation in your life and every interaction you have with someone is a form of initiation that allows you to either remain as you are or to evolve into your highest potential as a human being and a spiritual being and make a beautiful difference in the world.

So let's do this.

Let's heal this world.

Let's activate our hearts and flow love into this world.

Let's connect.

Please share your stories.

Please share your everyday initiations.

This book started by me writing the stories that I have lived and then I shared them on social media and in my newsletters.

These stories are what across the boards are the most popular things I share.

Clearly, stories of connection and everyday initiations are what people most need to hear.

There are countless times that people have told me that these stories have positively changed their lives.

You telling your stories and your everyday initiations will positively impact the lives of those that you share them with too.

I am visioning that someday we will meet and will initiate each other by cocreating a magical story of connection together.

Until then, know that we are part of an amazing movement of love and connection.

Remember, positively transforming our world is quite simple.

It begins with you.

It begins with your beautiful heart.

It begins with love.

Let's initiate the world into greater love and connection.

In truth love is who we all truly are and it is what matters most.

I love you and I support you.

ACKNOWLEDGMENTS

Each and every one of these Everyday Initiations stories were the result of me being in the presence of extraordinary people, places and things that helped co-create them with me. I am grateful for you all. I am grateful that you showed up fully for life and for me. You are all magic-makers.

I am incredibly grateful for Gay Hendricks, for believing in me and the gift of my writing and for encouraging me to write this book, for shepherding me through the process of creating it and for introducing me to all of the amazing folks at Waterside Publishing.

I am grateful for my Mom Alice who has always encouraged me to write and for my Dad Eric who is definitely working behind the scenes in the Spirit World to help make a lot of magic manifest in my life.

I have many incredible friends, students and clients who have loved, supported and encouraged me and my writing every step of the way. Thank you for every "like", "love" and comment on my stories on social media and in my newsletters. Special thanks to some wonderful cheerleaders including Sam, Lisa, Susan, Zoe, Lais, Amy, Fred, Ina, Josette, Christabel, Lor, Elle, William, Douglas, Barbara all the fine folks at the Church of Trader Joe's, my Soul Family at The Esalen Institute, Abe and everyone in The Santa Barbara Bucket Brigade, and everyone in THE CREATORS groups.

I am so grateful for Waterside Publishing and to each and every team member who has made my dream of publishing this book a reality.

Thank you Cadence for taking the epic book cover photo and for all the lovely photos you have ever taken of me.

Thank you Alexey for "getting" my vision for the book cover and for co-creating it with me.

Big Love and Gratitude flowing to everyone everywhere who is doing everything in your power to be your best Self every moment.

I love you and support you.

RESOURCES AND CONTINUING EDUCATION

Please visit

www.annevandewater.com

to learn more about
the many resources and continuing education
that Anne has created to love and support you

ABOUT THE AUTHOR

Anne Van de Water has been a prolific writer since childhood.

She writes inspirational true stories about real people, places, things and experiences.

She is a true humanitarian, a champion and cheerleader for you to activate your highest potential as a human being and a Soul.

She is a Spiritual Teacher and Light Worker and is here to support fellow Light Workers, Leaders, Teachers, Entrepreneurs, Healers, Creatives and Change Makers make a positive contribution to humanity and our amazing planet.

Her mission is to help you clear the stress, tension and heavy energy in your life that is the result of living out of alignment with who you truly are and what is most important to you.

Her zone of mastery is to help you raise the vibration of your body, mind, heart, Soul and Spirit so you can manifest and embody your personal Vision for your life while bringing your beautiful gifts into the world in the most powerful, healthy and sustainable way possible.

Her intention is to support you in transforming your life into a reality that makes you enthusiastically and honestly feel that you are living an authentic, one of a kind and truly fulfilling existence.

Anne is based in her hometown of Santa Barbara, California and travels the world connecting with and cocreating inspirational stories with everyone and everything in her presence.

Visit her at www.annevandewater.com

www.ingramcontent.com/pod-product-compliance
Lightning Source LLC
Chambersburg PA
CBHW022006090426
42741CB00007B/910